PRACTICE MAKES PERFECT

Preparation for
State Reading
Assessments

LEVEL

Prestwick House

P.O. Box 658 Clayton, Delaware 19938

www.prestwickhouse.com

Senior Editor: Paul Moliken

Author: Cheryl Miller Thurston

Editor: Darlene Gilmore

Cover Design: Larry Knox

Production: Jeremy Clark

Prestwick House

LITERARY TOUCHSTONE CLASSICS™

P.O. Box 658 • Clayton, Delaware 19938
Tel: 1.800.932.4593
Fax: 1.888.718.9333
Web: www.prestwickhouse.com

ISBN 978-1-62019-008-1

PRACTICE MAKES PERFECT **LEVEL** 6

Preparation for
State Reading
Assessments

Table of Contents

State Reading Assessments

Introduction to the Student

LEVEL

How to Take a Reading Comprehension Test

Taking a reading comprehension test does not have to be a stressful event. The following tips and methods can be used to make your test-taking efforts more effective and your results more accurate.

FOCUS:

When you read a comprehension passage, you should try to identify the following:

- main idea ○ author's attitude or tone ○ author's purpose

Many comprehension questions focus on your ability to determine what the author is trying to say and why he or she is saying it. Think about whether the author is biased: Does he or she support, criticize, or remain objective about the subject? What clues show the author's attitude?

While you read, you should imagine yourself as the test writer.

- Which pieces of information do you think are important?
- Is the passage about a person or a group of people?
- What is that person's or group's message to the world?
- What questions would you write about the passage?

When you come across a point that stands out, make a mental note of it. Ask yourself why the author included it. Information that seems to have a special purpose often shows up in the questions.

TIPS:

In order to determine an author's attitude toward the subject, look for emotionally charged words, such as *tragically, sadly, unfortunately, surprisingly, amazingly, justly,* etc. These words indicate an author's bias—whether the author sides with or against the subject of the passage. Simple words tell you a lot about the author's feelings.

Frequently, you are asked to identify the main idea of a passage. These types of questions do not always use the words *main idea.* They may ask for the most appropriate title or the statement with which the author would most likely agree or disagree. Pick the answer that is true for the entire passage. If no choice relates to the entire selection, choose the answer that is supported by most of the passage.

You will also encounter questions that ask you to define a word or find the most appropriate synonym. These questions check your ability to use context clues, not your vocabulary knowledge. Sometimes, you will find more than one seemingly correct answer, but when you look at the word as it is used in the paragraph, you can choose the best synonym for the situation.

Some questions are open-ended and require you to write an answer. You must write two-to-four complete sentences to answer these types of questions. The person who scores your answer will look for you to explain yourself, so be sure to support your opinion with details from the passage.

Finally, when it comes to taking timed tests, many people feel pressured to race through the work so that they complete all of it. Remember, though, that careful reading cannot be rushed. So, what can you do? When you cannot decide the answer to a question, skip it and come back to it after you have answered the rest of the questions for that passage. You may even find the answer when you are working on other questions. If you still cannot answer it, make your best guess and move on, rather than spend too much time trying to figure out one question, leaving yourself insufficient time to answer the rest accurately.

Some people suggest reading the questions before you read the passage so that you know what information you need. If this works for you, that is terrific! For many people, however, this uses valuable time and results in too much information to remember. This breaks their concentration, and they cannot focus on what they read. If you cannot focus on both the questions and the reading at one time, read the passage first, concentrating on what you read. If you need to look back at the passage to answer the questions, go ahead and do so. The point to be made here is that you should work in a manner that is comfortable for you. When you find a technique that works for you, use it!

REMEMBER THESE THREE EXTREMELY IMPORTANT POINTS:

1. **Read the passage and answer the questions that follow it!**
   Look for tricky words, such as *not, always, true, opposite*, etc. These words greatly affect the answer to the question.

2. **If you cannot remember what you just read, read it again, and pay attention to it!**

3. **Always read all the answer choices!**
   You may choose the wrong answer and miss the correct one entirely if you stop reading once you think you have found the answer. There may be a better choice further down the list, and you will miss it if you do not read it.

Model Passage

The following model passage demonstrates effective use of the reading tips and strategies. You will see that there are underlined words and phrases in the passage and notes in the margins. The notes in the margins refer to the underlined portions of the passage and serve as examples of the way you should think about the passage. These notes include questions you should ask yourself or comments you should make to yourself as you read.

The Railroads Connect

[1]This passage will be about the disorder of the "Wedding of the Rails" celebration.

On May 10, 1869, the Transcontinental Railroad was finally connected after years of hard work and confusion, but the celebration of the "Wedding of the Rails" was plagued by disorder and misunderstanding.[1]

[2]What are the funny errors?

[3]The points are organized. The word *first* tells me to look for *second*, etc. Look for *next* and *finally*.

[4]Wow, that is only six days before the ceremony.

[5]Wow, $400 of his own gold! Why? What kind of question could the test ask about this?

[6]I should look at the context of these boldfaced words. What do they mean?

[7]Those spikes were just dropped in the holes!

[8]This was a huge event if the telegraph was going to relay the sound.

Of course, the real story is a comedy of errors.[2] First,[3] the actual location of the event was Promontory Summit, Utah, but since this was not on the map, the press reported that it occurred at Promontory Point; therefore, postcards, souvenirs, and even textbooks to this day bear the name of the incorrect location. Second, on May 4, 1869,[4] the president of the Central Pacific Railroad, Leland Stanford, revealed to his friend, David Hewes, that no commemorative item had been made for the event. Upset by this fact, Hewes attempted to have a solid gold rail made, but after failing to find someone to finance it, he had $400 worth of his own gold melted and cast[5] as the "Golden Spike," which was then **engraved**[6] for the occasion. Three other spikes were also made for the event. The next problem arose when the event had to be postponed because **disgruntled**[6] workers and poor weather conditions delayed the arrival of officials from the Union Pacific Railroad. Finally, on May 10, 1869, the officials from both the Union Pacific and the Central Pacific railroads **convened** for the celebration. A special laurelwood railroad tie was laid in place at the junction, and the specially-made spikes were dropped into pre-drilled holes. Not one of them was actually hammered into place.[7] Then, the laurelwood tie and spikes were replaced with a standard tie and regular iron spikes. The last spike and the hammer were connected to the telegraph line so that the entire nation could hear[8] the "Wedding of the

[9]The name of the event is mentioned again. This must be important.

[10]That is funny—after all of the problems, the important people who were supposed to hammer the spike could not do it.

[11]That is funny, too. I cannot believe no one showed up. It seems as if no one cared.

Rails."[9] The sound of the hammer hitting the spike would then travel across the country through the telegraph line. Leland Stanford was given the first swing, but he missed[10] the spike and hit the wooden tie. Thomas Durant, vice president of the Union Pacific Railroad, swung at the spike, but missed entirely. In the end, a railroad employee hammered in the final tie,[10] and the telegraph operator sent the message to the country: "D-O-N-E."

Not so surprisingly, when the fiftieth anniversary celebration was scheduled, not one person showed up.[11] Maybe they all went to Promontory Point.

1. Which of the following best states the author's purpose?
- **A.** to make fun of the Transcontinental Railroad
- **B.** to make an accurate portrayal of an important event in railroad history
- **C.** to explain the importance of the Golden Spike
- **D.** to describe how history books sometimes contain incorrect information

(B) *The author accurately describes the confusion and mishaps surrounding the "Wedding of the Rails" celebration. All other answer choices are merely supporting points in the passage.*

2. Which of the following would be the best title for this passage?
- **A.** The Golden Spike Disaster
- **B.** Where the Railroads Meet
- **C.** Leland Stanford's Spike
- **D.** The Wedding of the Rails

(D) *The passage is about the entire "Wedding of the Rails" ceremony. After all, the ceremony's title is mentioned twice in the passage, making it significant information and appropriate for the title. Although the event was riddled with errors, it would not be considered a disaster. Finally, the passage does not focus solely on Leland Stanford's spike or where the event occurred.*

3. Which of the following did not contribute to the confusion on May 10, 1869?
   A. the telegraph operator
   B. poor weather conditions
   C. last-minute planning
   D. uncertainty about the location

(A) The telegraph operator did not make any errors. The poor weather postponed officials, last minute planning required a friend to donate his own gold for the commemorative spike, and uncertainty about the location led to incorrect information.

4. As used in the passage, the word *engraved* most nearly means
   A. molded.
   B. decorated.
   C. transported.
   D. purchased.

(B) If the spike was <u>engraved</u> for the occasion, it must have been decorated to show its commemorative purpose. <u>Molded</u> is not the answer because the passage already stated that the gold was melted and cast. Although the spike would have to be <u>transported</u>, the context is discussing the making of the spike, not the shipping of the spike. Finally, the gold was already <u>purchased</u> since it belonged to Hewes.

5. Based on the information provided in the passage, what can you infer is the reason for David Hewes's melting his own gold to make the spike?
   A. He was angry that no one would help him.
   B. He wanted to become famous for his contribution to the Transcontinental Railroad.
   C. He could find no one willing to pay for or donate the gold.
   D. He had more gold than he needed, so he was willing to give some away.

(C) Hewes tried to find someone to finance a rail but was unsuccessful. Had he found someone willing to pay or donate at least something, then he would not have had to use his own resources. Since he looked for someone to finance a golden rail instead of financing it himself, we can infer that he did not have an overabundance of gold. There are no clues to imply he was searching for fame. Finally, the passage states that he was upset that there was no item made to commemorate the event, but no mention of his being angry at finding no one willing to help.

6. *Answer the following question using complete sentences:*

  Why does the author call the "Wedding of the Rails" a "comedy of errors"?

The event is humorous because it was a major celebration of the uniting of the country's rails, which was a massive undertaking, and almost everything that could go wrong did. Railroad officials arrived late because their workers were unhappy, the commemorative spike was not even hammered in, and a railroad employee, not any of the officials who organized the celebration, completed the actual connection of the rails. As a final taunt, no one showed up for the fiftieth anniversary celebration.

Sputnik

TODAY, THE UNITED STATES and Russia are on friendly terms. However, on October 4, 1957, the relationships were a lot different. Russia was then part of the Soviet Union, a communist dictatorship. When the Soviet Union successfully sent a satellite called *Sputnik* into orbit around the earth, the United States was stunned. If the Soviets had the technology to send a satellite into space, what else could they do? Did they have advanced rockets that might carry a nuclear weapon? Were they planning conquests of planets or the moon? Fear and doubt swept the nation. Months after *Sputnik's* launch, a Gallup Poll showed that 60% of Americans thought that the countries were ready for an all-out nuclear war.

A month later, the Soviets sent *Sputnik* 2 into space. This larger satellite carried a female dog named Laika into orbit, but there was no re-entry plan, and she died in space. People around the world were outraged, but Laika did give Russian scientists the first information about how a living organism behaves in space.

On January 31, 1958, the U.S. had its first success with the launch of the satellite called *Explorer 1*. However, what became known as the "Space Race" was just beginning. For many years, the U.S. and the Soviet Union competed, with each trying to show its **dominance** through that country's achievements in exploring and understanding the mysteries of space. Winning the "Space Race" would be a great boost for the U.S. scientifically, as well as politically, since it would prove that capitalism works better than communism.

The competition led to improved science education in America so that the U.S. would eventually surpass the Soviets. More money was poured into science, which led to the development of technologies we depend on today. For example, the Internet, cell phones, global positioning systems (GPS), and high-definition televisions were all developed first by NASA. Soon, plans were underway to try to reach the moon. In 1961, President John F. Kennedy said, "I believe that this nation should commit itself to achieving the goal, before this decade is out, of landing a man on the moon and returning him safely to the earth."

The efforts were successful. The space race started by *Sputnik* effectively ended on July 20, 1969, when U.S. astronaut Neil Armstrong became the first man to walk on the moon. ●

QUESTIONS

1. **According to the passage, which statement best sums up Americans' main reaction to the launching of *Sputnik*?**
   - **A.** People thought the Soviet treatment of animals was cruel.
   - **B.** People were worried that the Soviet Union might attack the U.S.
   - **C.** People thought that attack was just a public relations stunt.
   - **D.** People wanted the U.S. to attack the Soviet Union as soon as possible.

2. **As used in the passage, the word *dominance* most nearly means**
   - **A.** advanced qualities.
   - **B.** technological failures.
   - **C.** form of government.
   - **D.** military strength.

3. **Based on information given in the passage, which statement is true, when you compare the U.S. to the Soviet Union in 1957?**
   - **A.** The Soviet Union was closer to being able to land a man on the moon.
   - **B.** The U.S. had stronger laws against cruelty to animals.
   - **C.** The U.S. was training far more scientists in colleges and universities.
   - **D.** The Soviet Union demonstrated superiority in exploring outer space.

4. **Which of the following was *not* a result of the "Space Race"?**
   - **A.** More money was spent to develop technology.
   - **B.** Science education was improved in U.S. schools.
   - **C.** The U.S. successfully landed a man on the moon.
   - **D.** The Soviet Union was quickly able to launch *Sputnik 3*.

5. **What made the "Space Race" between the U.S. and the Soviet Union more than just an innocent competition?**
   - **A.** Communism and capitalism are completely opposite systems.
   - **B.** There was the danger that the Soviets might use a nuclear weapon.
   - **C.** Scientific advances would improve one country, but not the other.
   - **D.** No one knew what the outcome of the "Space Race" would be.

6. *Answer the following question using complete sentences:*
   Based on information in the article, why were Americans eager to be the first to land on the moon?

Grizzly Bears

WHEN I RECENTLY VISITED Glacier National Park in the northwest corner of Montana, I was surprised to hear other hikers talking about wearing something called *bear bells*. My hiking partner and I knew that the park is home to grizzly bears, so we started asking questions and learned some very interesting facts about one of the largest land animals in North America.

Grizzly bears, it seems, don't want to encounter a person any more than a person wants to run into them. Though experts **scoff** at how silly the idea is, it is commonly believed that bells worn on clothing will warn bears of approaching humans and give them time to leave. In reality, the bells probably don't do much good because the bears can't hear them if there is noise like wind or rushing water.

People tend to feel a combination of both fear and fascination about grizzly bears. They would love to see a wild grizzly because grizzlies are impressive wonders of nature. On the other hand, the bears are extremely dangerous if they need to protect either their cubs or their source of food. They have powerful, humped shoulders and long, curved claws; they are also huge—often 6-7 feet tall when standing and weigh 400-800 pounds.

Grizzly bears hunt fish and small mammals, but they also eat almost anything they can find—up to 90 pounds a day in the fall when preparing for the winter, when the bears hibernate. Pregnant females do not even wake up to give birth; only a very few animals are able to do this. A mother typically has two blind and hairless cubs, each about the size of a chipmunk. They instinctively know how to nurse, and by the time their mother wakes up in the spring, they are strong enough to walk. She protects them for about three years, until they are able to feed on their own.

Because their population had shrunk, grizzlies were declared an endangered species by the U.S. Fish and Wildlife Service in 1975, and it is now illegal to harm a grizzly in any way. Thanks to this law, the population of grizzly bears has increased to about 30,000, and they no longer face a threat of extinction. ●

QUESTIONS

1. **As used in the second paragraph, *scoff* most nearly means**
    - **A.** publicize or tell about.
    - **B.** respect or honor.
    - **C.** wonder or puzzle about.
    - **D.** mock or make fun of.

2. **Which of the following is *not* true about grizzly bears?**
    - **A.** They have been designated an endangered species.
    - **B.** They hunt humans and are quite aggressive toward them.
    - **C.** They hibernate throughout the cold winter months.
    - **D.** Some of them live in Glacier National Park in Montana.

3. **What can you infer is the reason that grizzly bears eat so much food in the fall?**
    - **A.** They prefer the kinds of foods available to them in the fall.
    - **B.** They are stocking up, preparing their bodies for hibernation.
    - **C.** They use up a lot of energy helping their cubs exercise and grow.
    - **D.** They are eating because grizzlies are usually hungry.

4. **According to the passage, which of the following is true about bear bells?**
    - **A.** They are very effective at warning bears of approaching humans.
    - **B.** Bears probably can't hear bear bells over the sounds of the forest.
    - **C.** Forest rangers wear them on their hiking boots for protection.
    - **D.** Grizzly bears hear the bells, but usually tend to ignore them.

5. **According to the passage, why were grizzly bears designated an endangered species?**
    - **A.** Their population had seriously declined.
    - **B.** They were dangerous to people hiking.
    - **C.** They needed to be moved away from farms.
    - **D.** Their eating habits ruined the areas they lived in.

6. *Answer the following question using complete sentences:*
    The author mentions that grizzly bears are "impressive wonders of nature." What do you think the author means by that phrase?

Levi Strauss

On January 24, 1848, a man working in northern California found a piece of yellowish rock at a place called Sutter's Mill. Within a year, 300,000 prospectors, soon called "forty-niners," since that's the year most of them arrived, were searching in California to find riches beyond their wildest dreams in what came to be known as the Gold Rush.

Living conditions, however, were not easy. Most men—women who searched for gold were rare—lived in tents in the hills or near rivers. They struggled every day to find the vein of gold that would make them millionaires. Not many did, though. Most of them left poor and tired. However, a few men made their fortunes because of the Gold Rush anyway.

Samuel Brannan supplied the forty-niners with everything they needed to search for gold: horses, shovels, axes, food, and general supplies. In one month, his store sold over $150,000 worth of mining goods. Philip Armour made enough money in the gold fields to begin his Armour Meat Packing company. James Lick sold chocolate to prospectors, made a fortune in land sales, and when he died, he was the richest man in California. While you may not have heard of these men, you probably do know Levi Strauss.

Strauss became part of the Gold Rush when he was twenty years old. The Strauss family owned a store in San Francisco that sold clothing, umbrellas, fabric, and other goods to miners. This **venture** made him a little extra money, but it wasn't until 1872 that the company really expanded. The weakest parts of the pants Levi Strauss was making were the pockets. Carrying anything heavy made the seams come undone, so Strauss and a new partner began putting metal rivets in the corners of all the pants pockets. A business legend was born that continues today. When Levi Strauss died in 1902, he left his family a company worth $6,000,000.

In the twentieth century, many famous people began wearing jeans, and Levi's benefited from this popularity. In 2011, a pair of genuine antique Levi's sold for $150,000, and that year, Levi's, those simple blue denim jeans, the invention of an immigrant and his partner, grossed over two billion dollars. It is now an international company, but is based in America, and still produces jeans with rivets in them. ●

QUESTIONS

1. **What is the purpose of the final paragraph?**
   A. to encourage people to sell their antique jeans for lots of money
   B. to show how famous celebrities can influence what people buy
   C. to show how a small company grew into a large, successful one
   D. to detail how any small business can grow into an international business

2. **As used in the passage, *venture* most likely means**
   A. deal.
   B. business.
   C. adventure.
   D. attempt.

3. **What were the people who searched for gold nicknamed?**
   A. forty-niners
   B. miners
   C. gold rushers
   D. Levi's

4. **According to the passage, which statement about the pockets of jeans is correct?**
   A. They became torn because of the sharp tools the miners used.
   B. They were not deep enough to hold the tools miners needed.
   C. Gold fell through them, so the pockets were made thicker.
   D. The seams ripped due to things the miners carried in them.

5. **What is the main purpose of the paragraph that mentions the men who did get rich during the Gold Rush?**
   A. to show that three men made huge fortunes in California in that time
   B. to show that fortunes were not all made from prospecting for gold
   C. to show how one person increased his wealth by selling chocolate
   D. to show the three men as being very much wiser than the miners were

6. *Answer the following question using complete sentences:*
   The first three paragraphs are about very different topics than the final two are. Explain why you think that might be.

Tenzing Norgay: Man of Everest

IS IT POSSIBLE FOR ANYONE to survive on top of Mount Everest? Because the mountain is over 29,000 feet high, people weren't sure that a human being would have enough oxygen to breathe at that altitude. No one really knew the answer to that question—until Tenzing Norgay and Sir Edmund Hillary, a New Zealand climber, reached the summit in 1953.

Tenzing Norgay grew up in a valley near Mount Everest, which is located on the border between Nepal and Tibet in Asia. He was born a Sherpa, a Tibetan tribe that lives in the Himalayas and is well known for providing support for mountain climbing expeditions; Sherpas carry supplies and serve as guides. Norgay was originally named Namgyal Wangdi, but his name was changed when his family took him to visit a Buddhist monastery, and a monk said his name should be changed to Tenzing Norgay, which means "Wealthy Fortunate Follower of Religion."

Norgay always had a fascination with Mount Everest, and by the time he was 39, he had been a part of six expeditions that tried, but never **ascended** to the peak of the world's highest mountain.

In the spring of 1953, he joined a new expedition funded by the British.

The climbers spent many weeks on the mountain getting used to the altitude. They would stay at one camp for a week or two, move higher, stay there, then climb to an even higher elevation. When they reached the last camp, at over 25,000 feet above sea level, they camped for the final time.

After a severe snowstorm, Norgay and Hillary set off for the summit, stopping now and then to clear ice from the breathing tubes on the oxygen tanks they carried. After overcoming freezing temperatures and fierce winds, they at last reached the summit, where Hillary took photos of Norgay. When questioned later about why Norgay didn't take photos of him, he explained that Tenzing did not know how to operate the camera, and the conditions were too severe for a lesson.

The news of Norgay and Hillary's success made them enormously famous. Although he never learned to write, Norgay could speak several languages and later worked with a writer on a book about his life called *Man of Everest*. Tenzing Norgay died in 1986. ●

QUESTIONS

1. **The passage mentions that both Tenzing Norgay and Sir Edmund Hillary reached the summit of Mount Everest. However, the focus is on Norgay. Which statement best describes the author's reason for not including more about Hillary?**
   A. Norgay was more important than Hillary in making the expedition successful.
   B. Hillary's picture was not taken at the top, so some think he didn't really make it.
   C. The purpose of the passage is to tell about Tenzing Norgay, not Sir Edmund Hillary.
   D. Norgay was a stronger climber than Hillary and reached the top first.

2. **As used in the passage, what does *ascended* most nearly mean?**
   A. conquered; fought
   B. moved higher; rose
   C. investigated; discovered
   D. dreamt of; imagined

3. **Based on the passage, which of the following is true about Norgay?**
   A. He was a Buddhist.
   B. He was English.
   C. He died young.
   D. He had several children.

4. **Which of the following can be inferred about Norgay, based on the passage?**
   A. He converted to Christianity in later life.
   B. He originally wanted to become a farmer.
   C. He was quite strong and physically fit.
   D. He studied Buddhist writings at night.

5. **Which statement best describes why the author includes the detail about Norgay and Hillary clearing ice from the breathing tubes on the oxygen tanks they carried?**
   A. to show the difficult conditions the two endured on their climb
   B. to emphasize the importance of oxygen tanks in reaching the top
   C. to lessen their accomplishment because they had to use oxygen
   D. to emphasize the weight the two had to carry on their journey

6. *Answer the following question using complete sentences:*
   The passage mentions that Norgay could speak several languages. Based on this fact, what else do you think can be assumed about Norgay?

Paralympics

WHENEVER THE OLYMPICS are held, another competition is held alongside them: the Paralympics. The Paralympics is an event for world-class athletes who have some type of physical impairment. Athletes are classified in groups, according to the type and extent of their disabilities. Competitors may include athletes with cerebral palsy, missing limbs, or other physical problems, such as blindness or deafness. More than 25 sports are now included, such as rugby, judo, skiing, hockey, volleyball, and cycling.

The word *Paralympics* comes from the Greek word *para*, meaning "equal to" or "alongside," as in "parallel." It has nothing to do with the word *paralyzed*, as many people believe. Instead, the name indicates that the two competitions exist side-by-side and are equally important. In addition, the Paralympic Games should not be confused with the Special Olympics, which is for adults and children who are mentally challenged.

Tatyana McFadden is just one of the hundreds of Paralympians who have inspired others with success at the Games. Tatyana was born in Russia with a condition known as spina bifida. She had a hole in her spine, which has been repaired. An underdeveloped spinal cord and paralysis below the waist are two of her other permanent disabilities. Her parents sent her to an orphanage that was so poor it could not even afford crayons for the children. A wheelchair for Tatyana was impossible, so she spent six years walking on her hands since that was the only way she could move around.

In 1994, a woman named Debbie McFadden visited the orphanage on a business trip, met Tatyana, decided to adopt her, and brought her to the United States. Tatyana tried just about every sport she could in order to build up her strength—ping pong, archery, and basketball. However, she quickly fell in love with wheelchair racing, and by the age of 15, Tatyana was the youngest member of the USA track and field team at the Athens Paralympic Games. She surprised everyone by winning two medals and has continued to bring home silver, gold, and bronze medals at each **subsequent** competition.

With more and more media coverage of the Games, people all over the world have been able to watch and marvel at the success of athletes such as Tatyana McFadden and other Paralympic stars from all over the world. Few other athletes have accomplished what she has, though. ●

QUESTIONS

1. **Which of the following best states the author's purpose?**
   A. to help the reader feel sympathy for athletes with disabilities
   B. to inform the reader about the Paralympic games and Paralympians
   C. to tell about Tatyana McFadden and her difficult start in life
   D. to encourage readers to watch Paralympic games on television

2. **According to the passage, which athletes are *not* allowed to compete in the Paralympics?**
   A. athletes who are mentally challenged
   B. athletes who are visually impaired
   C. athletes who have missing limbs
   D. athletes who have cerebral palsy

3. **As used in the passage, what does *subsequent* most likely mean?**
   A. taking place in a foreign country
   B. simultaneous; at the same time
   C. competing at a lower level
   D. occurring next; following

4. **Which would be the best title for this article?**
   A. McFadden and the Paralympics
   B. The Disabled and the Paralympics
   C. How Paralympics Helped
   D. The History of the Paralympics

5. **Which set of words would best describe Tatyana McFadden?**
   A. self-centered, serious, disabled
   B. competitive, young, angry
   C. depressed, athletic, lucky
   D. strong, resourceful, competitive

6. *Answer the following question using complete sentences:*
   Why do you think the Paralympics and the Special Olympics are separate competitions? Explain.

Krakatoa

THE LOUDEST SOUND EVER heard by human beings throughout all of recorded history is thought to be the noise made in 1883 by the enormous eruption of Krakatoa, a volcano located in the ocean around Indonesia. The explosion was so loud that it was heard over 2,000 miles away. The explosive force was many times greater than the force of the nuclear bomb dropped on Hiroshima in World War II.

The eruption was preceded by several months of small explosions, escaping steam, earthquakes, and other disturbances, **culminating** in the major explosion on August 27th that sent ash 50 miles high and plunged the whole area into darkness for two and a half days.

No one is thought to have lived on Krakatoa itself, but the force of the volcano set off tsunamis that destroyed 165 nearby coastal villages and damaged 135 more, killing more than 36,000 people. The biggest wave, occurring soon after Krakatoa blew up, reached a height of 120 feet—about as high as a twelve-story building. Tsunamis also occurred as far away as Hawaii and South America, and ships in South Africa rocked from the waves. Ash from the eruption traveled around the globe, affecting weather and lowering temperatures around the world for many years. Krakatoa was almost completely destroyed. Water covered where it had once been.

One eyewitness account of the Krakatoa disaster comes from a Dutch woman named Johanna Beyerinck, who lived in a coastal village 25 miles north of Krakatoa; her husband was in charge of a Dutch colony there. She wrote of her terrible experiences during and after the explosion. A tsunami that was caused by Krakatoa's destruction struck the family's house, destroying much of it, and Mrs. Beyerinck, her husband, and three children made it to a hut they owned located in a higher area. Soon, they saw fires everywhere and then were hit with a fast-moving current of very hot gas and burning rocks. Rocks actually can melt and can even explode if enough heat is applied. The family was severely burned; Mrs. Beyerinck later described her arms and legs as swelling to three times their normal size. Her 14-month-old baby died in her arms.

What is most interesting to scientists is that, at present, another Krakatoa is rising from the sea and will erupt at some time in the future. ⬤

QUESTIONS

1. **Which of the following did *not* occur after Krakatoa exploded?**
   - **A.** Tsunamis destroyed 165 nearby villages and damaged many more.
   - **B.** The area was plunged into darkness because of ash in the air.
   - **C.** Earthquakes and aftershocks traveled as far as South Africa.
   - **D.** Ash in the air caused weather and temperature changes for years.

2. **What is the most likely reason the author gives details about what happened to the Beyerincks?**
   - **A.** The author thinks the suffering of the Beyerincks was more important than the suffering of the natives.
   - **B.** The author hopes that details about what happened to real people will help readers understand the impact of Krakatoa.
   - **C.** The author wants to point out that natives blamed the eruption on the Dutch who had moved into the area.
   - **D.** The author wants to show that, despite the devastation of the volcano, some people were rescued by ships and survived.

3. **As used in the passage, what does the word *culminating* most likely mean?**
   - **A.** ending; arriving at the final stage
   - **B.** starting; beginning a series
   - **C.** hiding; cloaking in darkness
   - **D.** defining; setting the standard

4. **According to the passage, which of the following is true?**
   - **A.** Thousands of men, women, and children died on Krakatoa itself.
   - **B.** Krakatoa is thought to have been uninhabited at the time.
   - **C.** People moved back to Krakatoa within months of the explosion.
   - **D.** Damage on Krakatoa was actually not as bad as it was to nearby islands.

5. **What is the purpose of the third paragraph?**
   - **A.** to tell about the effects of Krakatoa on the world
   - **B.** to explain how Krakatoa affected the Beyerincks
   - **C.** to compare Krakatoa to the bombing of Hiroshima
   - **D.** to point out that tsunamis can be very dangerous

6. *Answer the following question using complete sentences:*
   Why do you think the author explains that 120 feet is about as high as a twelve-story building?

Hannibal and the Elephants

HANNIBAL, WHO LIVED from 247-182 BCE, is considered one of the greatest military commanders in history. He lived in the city-state of Carthage, located in northern Africa, and his greatest enemy in the world was the republic of Rome. When Hannibal was very young, his father supposedly made him swear on his life that he would always be an enemy of Rome.

When Hannibal was in his twenties, he came up with an **ingenious** plan for the army he led. Instead of attacking Rome by sea, which would be the most expected route, he decided to invade Rome by going through a difficult, snow-covered mountain range, the Alps, in order to get there. He gathered an army of 60,000 troops and, to help transport everything, 37 elephants.

The journey was complicated and seemed impossible at times. By the time Hannibal reached Italy, he had only 26,000 troops left. Still, his army won the first battle easily, partly because the Romans had a hard time dealing with the elephants. The Carthaginians would give the elephants large quantities of wine and then poke their heels to make them go mad. The elephants would go wild, charging into battle. Their massive size, along with their trumpeting, frightened Roman horses and made it difficult for the Romans to attack. Some historians say that the Romans had discovered that elephants are frightened by the sound of squealing pigs, so they would cover pigs in tar, light them on fire, and let them loose among the elephants. But, Hannibal counteracted this tactic by putting pigs in his elephant stables, allowing the huge beasts to get used to their squeals.

Most of Hannibal's elephants died from the cold weather soon after the first battle, but even without the elephants, Hannibal was able to soundly defeat the Romans in the next battle as well. Over 50,000 Romans died, along with 5,000 Carthaginians, and it appeared that the Romans would not be able to recover. They did not give in, though, and Hannibal and his men continued their assaults for another fifteen years, even attacking Rome itself. In the end, Hannibal was not able to defeat Rome.

Many years later, when he was 64, it became clear that Hannibal was going to be taken prisoner. He swallowed poison and killed himself rather than surrender to his sworn enemy, the Romans. ●

QUESTIONS

1. **Which statement best states the purpose of the third paragraph?**
   - **A.** to point out the difficulty of Hannibal's journey over the Alps
   - **B.** to explain why Hannibal had pigs sleep in the stables
   - **C.** to show how the elephants helped Hannibal win the first battle
   - **D.** to list the reasons that Hannibal was considered a great commander

2. **As used in the passage, the word *ingenious* most nearly means**
   - **A.** clever or brilliant.
   - **B.** simple or basic.
   - **C.** evil or monstrous.
   - **D.** silly or confusing.

3. **What promise did Hannibal supposedly make to his father?**
   - **A.** to become a great military leader
   - **B.** to always be an enemy of Rome
   - **C.** to conquer other countries besides Rome
   - **D.** to find a way to attack Rome by sea

4. **According to the passage, why did many of Hannibal's elephants die?**
   - **A.** They fell off high mountain passes.
   - **B.** They were stabbed by Roman lances.
   - **C.** They died from the cold weather.
   - **D.** They starved to death in the Alps.

5. **Which of the following summarizes why elephants were effective against the Romans?**
   - **A.** The Romans hated their terrible odor.
   - **B.** The elephants frightened the horses.
   - **C.** The elephants trampled many soldiers.
   - **D.** No weapons could hurt the elephants.

6. *Answer the following question using complete sentences:*
   Why do you think it would be difficult to take elephants across the Alps? Explain your answer in your own words.

The Bermuda Triangle

AN AREA OFF THE southeastern Atlantic coast of the United States has quite a reputation. Known informally as the "Bermuda Triangle," to some people, it is a place where ships and planes disappear for no reason. To others, it is not remarkable at all—except for the stories that surround it.

One of the most famous stories concerns the "ghost ship," the *Mary Celeste*, which was found floating without a crew in 1872. The ship appeared undamaged, and the cargo was **intact**; nothing was ruined or broken. In addition, there was enough food and water on board for six months. No one has ever figured out what happened to the crew members, but some have blamed their disappearance on mysterious forces in the Bermuda Triangle, even though the ship was found off the coast of Portugal—nowhere near the Bermuda Triangle. The problem may be that some people have confused the ghost ship with another ship, the *Maria Celestia*, which struck a reef off the coast of Bermuda in 1864 and sank.

The "supernatural" area got its name in 1964 when a magazine printed a story called "Bermuda Triangle." The article was about five U.S. Navy planes that left Florida on a routine training mission in 1945 and were never seen again. The name stuck, and from then on, stories and legends about the Triangle grew. People started telling about disappearances related to sea monsters, extraterrestrials, strange magnetic forces, and even giant quantities of methane suddenly bubbling up from the ocean. Weird theories still continue, but many scientists say the reality is more boring. Storms, human error, poor design of ships and planes, and bad luck may have more to do with the disappearances than anything else has.

In a 2003 *National Geographic News* article, a historian with the U.S. Naval Historical Foundation explained that the Bermuda Triangle is in a part of the ocean that has been a busy trading route for hundreds of years. He said, "To say quite a few ships and airplanes have gone down there is like saying there are lot of car accidents on the New Jersey Turnpike."

People love a good mystery, so the stories are likely to continue. The greatest mystery may be this: Is there really any mystery at all to the disappearances in the Bermuda Triangle? ◉

QUESTIONS

1. The author's main point is best described by which of the following statements?
- **A.** The Bermuda Triangle is one of the most unusual and mysterious places on the face of the earth.
- **B.** The Bermuda Triangle is probably responsible for the disappearance of the crew of the *Mary Celeste*.
- **C.** The mysteries surrounding the strange disappearances in the Bermuda Triangle may have logical explanations after all.
- **D.** The Bermuda Triangle mysteries are clearly hoaxes that intelligent people should never believe.

2. Which statement best reflects the point of the fourth paragraph?
- **A.** When a place has a lot of traffic, accidents are bound to happen.
- **B.** Magnetic forces in the Bermuda Triangle cause ships to sink.
- **C.** No one can explain the strange disappearances in the Bermuda Triangle.
- **D.** A *National Geographic News* historian solved the mystery of the Triangle.

3. As used in the passage, *intact* most likely means
- **A.** unbroken or whole.
- **B.** mysterious or strange.
- **C.** empty or missing.
- **D.** filled or complete.

4. Why is the *Mary Celeste* known as a "ghost ship"?
- **A.** It has been used in several horror movies.
- **B.** It was haunted by dead pirates.
- **C.** It was found with no one on board.
- **D.** It sunk because of ghostly influences.

5. What happened to the five planes that took off on a routine training mission in 1945?
- **A.** They crashed into the ocean.
- **B.** They were never seen again.
- **C.** They turned up near Portugal.
- **D.** They were shot down.

6. *Answer the following question using complete sentences:*
Do you think the author believes that the disappearances in the Bermuda Triangle are mysterious? Why or why not? Give evidence from the passage to support your answer.

Flying Discs

ALMOST EVERYONE HAS seen some sort of "flying saucer" floating to Earth in a field, backyard, or playground. This article, though, isn't about UFOs; it's about a toy that was first called a "flying disc." Most people, however, know the plastic toy as a *Frisbee*. There are other kinds of flying discs, but people tend to refer to all of them as "Frisbees."

Frisbee hasn't always been the name that was used, though. The man most responsible for the flying disc in its present form was Walter Frederick Morrison, an inventor. Morrison, who had tossed around many circular objects when he was young and watched them fly, worked on a few different designs until he developed a good flyer. He first called his plastic invention a *Whirlo-Way*, then, a *Flyin' Saucer*, and finally, a *Pluto Platter*.

How did a Pluto Platter come to be called a Frisbee? The full story begins in the 1870s when a Connecticut baker named William Russell Frisbie had an idea for marketing his pies. He had his last name embossed in the bottom of the reusable tin pans his company used as pie bottoms. He hoped people wanting to bake a pie would see the name and think, "It would be a whole lot easier just to buy a pie." The pies caught on and were soon sold all over Connecticut—including New Haven, where Yale University is located. In the 1940s, Yale students started tossing the pans to one another, using them as toys and as ways to have some outdoor exercise.

Morrison sold the rights to his own flying disc to the Wham-O company, which renamed the discs again, to *Frisbee* to honor its originator. The discs didn't really make the company a lot of money until around 1964, when they were redesigned so that they could be thrown more accurately. Sales soared, just as the discs do: More than 200 million have been sold.

Since then, many games and sports have been developed around flying discs, including disc golf, Ultimate, and disc dog. Disc dog competitions involve a handler and dog competing together in events such as distance and freestyle catching.

Today, when the weather is warm, a visitor to any public park in America is likely to see people, or people and their dogs, enjoying the carefree fun of tossing around the flying discs commonly known as Frisbees. ◗

QUESTIONS

1. **Where would you most likely find this article?**
    A. in a magazine about toy development
    B. in a blog offering advice on exercising
    C. in a research paper about Frisbees
    D. in a history of William Russell Frisbie's pies

2. **As used in the passage, _embossed_ most nearly means**
    A. sliced.
    B. taped.
    C. tied.
    D. stamped.

3. **Why did William Russell Frisbie have his name put on his pie pans?**
    A. He was someone who loved seeing anything about himself.
    B. He wanted people who saw the pans to think of his company.
    C. He wanted the pie tins returned so that he could re-use them.
    D. He hoped that they would become toys known by his name.

4. **Which of the following was _not_ an earlier name for what became the Frisbee?**
    A. Flyin' Saucer
    B. Pluto Platter
    C. Frisbie Disc
    D. Whirlo-Way

5. **Which statement is true about the flying disc, according to the article?**
    A. Many games have developed around the use of a flying disc.
    B. The flying disc was invented by Wham-O in around 1964.
    C. Students at Yale University invented the flying disc.
    D. A pie dish was originally thrown by Walter Morrison.

6. _Answer the following question using complete sentences:_
    What was Walter Frederick Morrison's involvement with the Frisbee, according to information you read in the passage?

The Snowflake Man

A SHY, QUIET VERMONT farmer named Wilson Bentley first became fascinated with water as a child—all forms of water, including dew, frost, clouds, rain, and snow. It was snowflakes, though, that captured his imagination, curiosity, and interest, not to mention his time and energy. When he was 15, his parents bought him a microscope, and he became fascinated with the beauty of ice crystals as they turn into snowflakes.

He tried to draw what he saw and made hundreds of sketches, but he knew that what he was drawing was inferior to what he was actually seeing. When he read about how cameras were being used to photograph objects through microscopes, he persuaded his parents to buy a camera, even though none of them knew anything about photography.

For over a year, Bentley experimented with the camera and, in 1885, finally managed to take the first photograph of a single snow crystal. He went on to take photos of more than 5,000 snowflakes, never finding two of them alike, and published a book called *Snow Crystals*, which contained more than 2,400 images of snowflakes photographed on a black background so that they would stand out. His book introduced the world to the complex beauty and uniqueness of snow crystals.

Bentley didn't limit his studies to snowflakes, however. In the summers, he turned to studying rain. He **theorized** that in order to figure out how rain is formed, he should start by measuring the size of raindrops. This idea needed to be tested, so he took a pan with flour about an inch deep and put it in the rain for several seconds. Each raindrop would soak up some flour and form a tiny pellet made of dough. When the pellets dried, Bentley measured their diameter. The simple measurement method he devised is still used today.

Eventually, Bentley wrote magazine articles telling others about the beauty he saw in the world of ice crystals, and he began to lecture to various organizations. He continued to make careful observations of the weather and document his findings. In 1924, the American Meteorological Society awarded Bentley a research grant in recognition of "40 years of extremely patient work." By then, he had become known simply as "The Snowflake Man." ●

QUESTIONS

1. **Wilson Bentley is best known for**
   - **A.** drawings he made of snowflakes.
   - **B.** showing what snowflakes look like.
   - **C.** taking the first photograph of snow.
   - **D.** publishing his book about snowflakes.

2. **Which statement would best describe how Bentley felt about snowflakes?**
   - **A.** He thought they were amazingly beautiful.
   - **B.** He was fascinated with how they fell.
   - **C.** He believed they were less interesting than raindrops.
   - **D.** He thought studying them might earn him a good income.

3. **As used in the passage, *theorized* most likely means**
   - **A.** planned.
   - **B.** estimated.
   - **C.** assumed.
   - **D.** wrote.

4. **Which of the following explains why Bentley started taking photographs of snowflakes?**
   - **A.** He wanted to publish a book on something important in the field of weather.
   - **B.** He was frustrated because his drawings didn't capture the beauty of snowflakes.
   - **C.** His parents thought he should try to make some money from his studies.
   - **D.** He wanted to begin lecturing and writing magazine articles on snowflakes.

5. **What is one contribution Bentley made to the study of rain?**
   - **A.** He photographed raindrops on black backgrounds.
   - **B.** He measured the amount of rainfall in various months.
   - **C.** He made drawings of raindrops under a microscope.
   - **D.** He figured out a practical way to measure the size of raindrops.

6. *Answer the following question using complete sentences:*
   People who pursue unusual ideas or interests have to overcome other people's criticism and negative opinions on the ideas and interests. This didn't happen with Bentley. Why might this have been the case? Explain your ideas in your own words.

Breaking the Sound Barrier

CHUCK YEAGER WAS A PILOT and a war hero in World War II; he flew 64 missions over Europe and shot down 13 German aircraft. History will remember him most, however, for being the first person to officially break the sound barrier. In other words, he flew a plane traveling faster than the speed of sound. How fast is that? Sound travels at just over 760 mph.

Military planes routinely break the sound barrier today, but in 1947, pilots weren't certain it could be

done. Pilots who had flown at speeds approaching the speed of sound had experienced problems with unstable controls and damage to their planes. Some thought that going faster than the speed of sound was impossible—that there was a "barrier," which might kill a person. Bell Aircraft Company, however, had built a new plane designed specifically for the purpose of breaking the sound barrier, and Chuck Yeager was asked to be on the team testing it.

Yeager flew on eight test flights, and his cool head under pressure allowed him to fly to safety after he encountered problems. The pilots and the engineers kept working on solutions to the problems, and finally, on October 14, 1947, he took his ninth run.

What those in charge didn't know at the time was that Yeager took this run with two broken ribs. He had been thrown from a horse two days earlier, and a doctor had taped his ribs. Yeager knew that he would never be allowed to fly with broken ribs, so he kept quiet about his injury. Broken ribs are very painful, but Yeager knew he could still fly the plane. What he couldn't do was pull the Bell X-1's side door into place and latch it. He explained his problem secretly to another test pilot, who created a **makeshift** handle out of a broomstick. Yeager tested it out on the ground and found he was able to use the stick to push the lever and lock the cockpit door.

On that trip, flying at an altitude of 43,000 feet at a top speed just a tiny bit above the speed of sound, Chuck Yeager officially broke the sound barrier in the X-1. The ground control operators heard what they thought was thunder in the distance, but it was actually a sonic boom—the sound made when an object exceeds the speed of sound. ●

QUESTIONS

1. The Bell X-1 was built for one specific purpose. What was it?

    A. to allow Yeager to test its abilities

    B. to be the fastest jet fighter in the world

    C. to fly faster than the speed of sound

    D. to fly at an altitude of 43,000 feet

2. As used in the passage, the word *makeshift* most nearly means

    A. temporary and not fancy.

    B. homemade and fragile.

    C. bendable but strong.

    D. wooden and risky.

3. The reader can infer that a "sonic boom" is something that can be

    A. harmful.

    B. big.

    C. bright.

    D. loud.

4. Why did some pilots assume it was impossible to break the sound barrier?

    A. Some planes completely disintegrated.

    B. The controls on some planes became unstable.

    C. Pilots sometimes became weightless.

    D. The wings on some planes shook.

5. What did Yeager do before working as a test pilot?

    A. He trained horses on a farm.

    B. He fought in World War II.

    C. He worked in a laboratory.

    D. He analyzed sonic booms.

6. *Answer the following question using complete sentences:*

What do you think is the author's purpose in explaining that Yeager flew with two broken ribs?

Not Just for Polkas

A PROFESSIONAL ACCORDION player recently took a poll, asking a number of people this question: "What do you think of when you hear the word *accordion*?" Almost everyone answered, "Polkas." Polkas are lively folk dances that are often associated with Austria, Poland, Germany, and other countries. Many people have heard polkas because this type of music is often played at wedding receptions.

What many people don't understand is that accordions are *not* just for polkas. Many accordionists play classical music, and a type of accordion called a bandoneón is popular in tango music. A button accordion is featured in conjunto music, which is especially popular in southern Texas and northern Mexico, and in zydeco music, which has its roots in southwestern Louisiana. A few popular rock bands also include an accordion.

The accordion's popularity in America probably reached its peak in the 1940s and early 1950s. Before television was invented, U.S. families spent a lot of time listening to the radio. In 1948, one popular show involved young people from all over the country competing week after week for a grand prize of $5,000. One contestant was a very handsome young Italian American named Dick Contino, who played the accordion. Although people couldn't see him on the radio, the teenage girls in the studio could, and they loved him. They stomped, yelled, and screamed his name as his fingers flew over the keys. Girls were **smitten**, and Contino finally won the grand prize.

Many believe that it was Contino's win that accounted for a dramatic increase in accordion sales. Suddenly, parents everywhere were signing their kids up for accordion lessons.

But then rock and roll came on the scene. Groups like the Beatles and the Rolling Stones featured drums and electric guitars, and teenagers wanted no part of the accordion. Many of them even started making fun of the instrument, and it began to disappear from popular music.

To young people growing up in the 1980s, though, the accordion was "new," and it started to make a comeback. People today may think they hear accordions only in polkas, but accordion music is everywhere—in commercials, movies, and many types of popular music. Even if people sometimes don't realize it, the accordion is becoming a popular instrument once again. ●

QUESTIONS

1. **Which of the following best states the purpose of the third paragraph?**
    A. to explain why the accordion became popular in the 1940s and early 1950s
    B. to point out the talent of a young accordionist named Dick Contino
    C. to show how radio used to influence people the way television does today
    D. to tell about how rock and roll groups helped popularize accordion music

2. **As used in the passage, *smitten* most likely means**
    A. surprised.
    B. puzzled.
    C. disgusted.
    D. charmed.

3. **What is a bandoneón?**
    A. a button accordion used in conjunto music
    B. a kind of folk dance from Austria
    C. a kind of accordion used in tango music
    D. a button accordion used in zydeco music

4. **Based on the passage, which of the following statements is true about the accordion?**
    A. Accordion music is heard today in commercials, movies, and all kinds of popular music.
    B. The one kind of music that accordionists never play is classical music.
    C. The accordion was especially popular among teenagers in the 1960s and 1970s.
    D. The best accordionists come from southwestern Louisiana and southern Texas.

5. **What can be inferred from the passage about Dick Contino?**
    A. He probably could have been successful in any field.
    B. His good looks probably had an influence on his popularity.
    C. He probably became very conceited because of all his success.
    D. His Italian heritage is probably what made him a great musician.

6. *Answer the following question using complete sentences:*
   Explain how the popularity of the Beatles and the Rolling Stones could have hurt the popularity of the accordion.

Where is the Green?

VISITORS TO THE MOUNTAIN areas of western North America are often in for an ugly surprise. Instead of the beautiful, dark green forests they expect, they see areas of brown and gray nearly everywhere they look—the result of millions of dead pine trees.

What has killed all these trees? A tiny insect about the size of a grain of rice has infected them with a disease. The mountain pine beetle is responsible for what may be the largest insect **blight** North America has ever seen.

Mountain pine beetles lay eggs under the bark of trees and inject a fungus that keeps the trees from fighting off the beetles. The fungus also cuts off nutrients and water, and the trees eventually die.

The cold winters in high mountain areas usually kill most of the beetle population and keep them from reproducing too rapidly. A temperature of at least 30 degrees below zero (Fahrenheit) for five days will kill a large number of beetle larva. But in recent years, the weather has been much warmer, and the beetles aren't dying off; in fact, they are multiplying at an enormous speed.

The beetles can actually be helpful to a forest. In normal years, they choose old and diseased trees, which die and make room for new and younger trees. But now, the beetles are reproducing more quickly and turning to healthy trees on which to lay their eggs. Millions of acres of trees have been lost.

What can be done? Once a tree is infected, nothing practical can be done to save it. Prevention is a better option. Some sprays have been developed, but because of the expense involved, they are useful mostly for small, targeted areas. There are also environmental concerns with some sprays, which can be dangerous for birds, mammals, other insects, and amphibians that live in or near the trees. No one yet knows the effect the sprays might have on humans.

The most effective way science has discovered to slow the spread is to find infected trees and destroy the beetles, in order to prevent them from spreading to more trees. With all the acres infected—ten times more than from previous infestations from other insects—that battle is a huge one. So far, the beetles are winning. ●

QUESTIONS

1. **Based on the passage, which of the following is true about pine beetle blight?**
   - **A.** Scientists have it under control in North America.
   - **B.** The warm weather from recent winters has helped control the blight.
   - **C.** Pine beetles inject a fungus that cuts off nutrients and water to a tree.
   - **D.** Sprays have been developed that can protect infected trees.

2. **As used in the passage, *blight* most likely means**
   - **A.** an outbreak of disease.
   - **B.** a very large swarm.
   - **C.** the offspring of pine beetles.
   - **D.** an attempt to kill beetles.

3. **According to the passage, which is the most effective way to deal with pine beetle blight?**
   - **A.** insecticides
   - **B.** prevention
   - **C.** burning
   - **D.** predators

4. **Which of the following statements best describe the author's purpose?**
   - **A.** to complain about the effect of the beetles on trees
   - **B.** to encourage more funding for efforts to destroy the beetles
   - **C.** to describe the problem of the pine beetle in North America
   - **D.** to point out the dangers of pine beetle blight to humans

5. **Which words best describes the pine beetle?**
   - **A.** hardy, reproductive
   - **B.** fragile, easily destroyed
   - **C.** large, strong
   - **D.** brown, spotted

6. ***Answer the following question using complete sentences:***
   What effect do you think pine beetle blight could have in the infected areas? Explain in your own words, but base your answer on the passage.

Rattlers—Killers or Not?

RATTLESNAKES HAVE a reputation as killers of humans. In Western movies, for example, it's very common to see a rattlesnake coiled and ready to strike, putting a cowboy's life in danger. But would his life really be in danger?

The answer is that the danger is not nearly as great as most people think. Although rattlesnake bites are very serious, few people actually die of them. More than 8,000 people are bitten each year, but many of those are zoo employees and others who handle snakes on a routine basis. Many others are people who have been teasing a snake for some reason or trying to capture or kill it. Of the 8,000 or so people bitten, there are only around 6-15 fatalities. Far more people die each year from other animal bites—for example, bites from rats, insects, or even dogs.

People often think of rattlesnakes as **aggressive** reptiles, but they are really rather timid and generally won't attack people unless they are cornered or frightened. We are too large for them to eat. However, if someone handles them incorrectly or bothers them in some way, they can and will strike. Their fangs are sharp, like needles, and inject as much as a teaspoon of venom when they bite.

Rattlesnakes hunt at night—usually rodents or lizards—when they don't have to depend on their vision. They have a small heat-sensing pit between their eyes and nostrils. This pit helps them sense live food in darkness because their victim has a different temperature than the air does. In the daylight hours, rattlesnakes hide, and when someone or something surprises them, they vibrate the rattles on the end of their tails, making a warning sound. Many of the people bitten each year have simply stepped on a log and surprised a snake.

In movies, rattlesnakes are usually shown coiled and ready to strike. People assume that the snake can strike only from this coiled position, but that is a myth. It can actually strike from just about any position and can even bite when moving or while underwater.

If you are walking or hiking in rattlesnake territory, it's smart to wear thick boots to protect against bites if you should accidentally surprise a rattlesnake. If you see or hear a rattlesnake, move away from it. Remember, it is afraid of you and is warning you with the rattling.

Finally, if a rattlesnake does bite you, don't panic. The bite is very painful, and you should seek medical help immediately, but it is unlikely to be fatal. ●

QUESTIONS

1. According to the passage, which statement is true?
    A. Rattlesnake bites are almost always fatal.
    B. Rattlesnake bites are painful, but not usually deadly.
    C. Rattlesnakes are most deadly when they are coiled.
    D. Rattlesnake bites are more dangerous than insect bites.

2. As used in the passage, the word *aggressive* most nearly means
    A. strong.
    B. forceful.
    C. odd.
    D. huge.

3. Which of the following best describes the author's purpose?
    A. to point out that rattlesnakes are not as dangerous as most people think
    B. to show that rattlesnakes can bite while underwater
    C. to compare rattlesnakes to rats
    D. to tell how to avoid rattlesnake bites

4. What are rattlesnakes' fangs compared to?
    A. needles
    B. teaspoons
    C. knives
    D. coils

5. Which statement is true?
    A. Rattlesnakes cause more deaths each year than dog bites do.
    B. Rattlesnakes are not afraid of people and will go to great lengths to bite them.
    C. Rattlesnakes most often bite children because children will get closer than adults will.
    D. People bitten by rattlesnakes have often been teasing it or trying to capture it.

6. *Answer the following question using complete sentences:*
Based on information in the article, in what two ways are rattlesnakes dangerous to people? Answer the question in your own words.

Maybe Someday

IMAGINE TRAVELING DOWN the freeway toward a distant city. You see trees, other cars, highway signs, buildings, the usual stuff. However, you are flying above the actual road, and the car is made entirely of glass. The trees are artificial; the other cars are not only beside you, but they are above and below yours also; the signs are in 3D; the buildings are all glass; and nobody is steering—the adults are all reading, eating, sleeping, or using their computers.

Lights on the car in front of you flash red, and your vehicle automatically slows down. But no one made it happen with a foot on the brake—it was all controlled by the computer in the glass-enclosed "Transportation Unit," the super-accurate regulator of traffic that surrounds all of this electro-magnetic travel. There are no accidents, no traffic jams, not even any bad weather. You are in a climate-controlled environment. These automated highways seem perfect. They allow travelers to conduct daily business, relax, or do whatever they want, while the so-called car transports them without any hassles.

You look up from your pre-packaged, delicious, freeze-dried hamburger, which is the size of a quarter, and see a moving 3D billboard showing a man in a suit with a jet-pack on his back going to work by flying through the clouds. You ask the personalized computer, the one that you carry all the time in the fabric of your clothing, to see another ad—it understands whatever you say to it.

This ad is for a completely hands-free house. All cooking, cleaning, lighting, temperatures, and maintenance is done by human-like robots that you program only once, and they perform their tasks **independently** from that moment on. You never need to touch them again.

A rocket-plane can take passengers from the United States to Europe in less than an hour, and for your next birthday, your favorite aunt has promised to take you on a week-long stay in the resort on the moon. There are even rumors that a vacation to Mars will be possible by the time you turn twenty.

When can you expect these wonderful human achievements? Well, they were all predicted at various World Fairs during the twentieth century, and they were all supposed to be available to the general population by 1975.

All I want to know is, "Where is my own jet pack?" ◉

QUESTIONS

1. **What definition would fit the best for the word** *independently***?**
   - **A.** without any hesitation
   - **B.** without any further human work
   - **C.** usually, but not always perfectly
   - **D.** with a great deal of speed

2. **What seems to be the author's purpose for the entire passage?**
   - **A.** to explain what the future of driving could be like
   - **B.** to show how many amazing products will be available
   - **C.** to demonstrate how predictions can sometimes be false
   - **D.** to make present-day readers jealous about the future

3. **Based on the author's comments, where did the inventions mentioned in the passage originate?**
   - **A.** in the author's imagination
   - **B.** at fairs in the last century
   - **C.** in a computer's memory
   - **D.** in an invention book written in 1975

4. **According to the article, how will trips be controlled in the future?**
   - **A.** They will be regulated by a computer in the "fabric of your clothing."
   - **B.** They will be able to take you to Europe in "less than an hour."
   - **C.** They will be controlled by a "Transportation Unit" around the road.
   - **D.** "Human-like robots" will take care of everything needed for travel.

5. **Which group of predictions about the future contains one item that is** *not* **covered in the article?**
   - **A.** computers, freedom from disease, robots
   - **B.** food, easy and safe transportation, space travel
   - **C.** programmable robots, home care, flying to work
   - **D.** artificial trees, moving billboards, all-glass buildings

6. *Answer the following question using complete sentences:*
   What do you think is the purpose of the final sentence of the passage?

The Invention of the Microwave Oven

IT IS ESTIMATED THAT nearly 90% of American households today have a microwave oven. It's a good thing these ovens have changed dramatically since they were first introduced, or kitchens would be very crowded. The first microwaves sold in 1947, weighed 750 pounds, and were about the same size as a modern refrigerator.

The invention of the microwave, however, came about by accident. In 1946, Dr. Percy Spencer was in a laboratory testing a new tube called a magnetron, which produces microwaves and is used in radar. Suddenly, he noticed that the candy bar in his pocket had melted. He was surprised and fascinated by this unexpected occurrence, so he experimented further, putting some popcorn kernels nearby. They popped all over the lab in a few minutes. The next day, he put an egg beside the magnetron, and the egg started wiggling around and shaking. A **colleague** wanted to be a witness to the experiment, so he bent toward the egg for a closer look. It quickly exploded, he ended up with hot egg all over his face, and could not work the rest of the day.

Dr. Spencer decided that he had discovered something important—that microwaves could be used to cook food rapidly. He created a metal box with a microwave connection and found that food cooked inside the box heated amazingly fast, much faster than foods heated on a stove or in an oven. Engineers went to work, and soon a microwave oven was being tested in a restaurant. Not long after that, the first commercial microwave was offered for sale.

How does a microwave oven actually heat food? It's a little complicated, but basically, the microwaves make molecules in the food move, and the friction causes heat. If you rub your hands together, you can feel the heat. It's almost the same process.

We take microwaves for granted today, but they were certainly odd when first introduced. People worried that the microwaves could cause blindness, radiation poisoning, or other diseases in humans, and it took time for the new type of oven to become popular. Improvements also helped. Microwaves became smaller, lighter, and cheaper, and by 1975, were outselling conventional gas ranges.

Soon, products were being invented just for the microwave oven—popcorn, dinners, and snacks became easy to cook in a microwave. People became hooked on the speed and convenience of a microwave oven, and cooking habits of Americans were changed forever. ●

QUESTIONS

1. **The invention of the microwave came about as a result of which of the following?**
   - **A.** a scientific experiment about molecules
   - **B.** a decade of debate among many scientists
   - **C.** an accidental discovery in a laboratory
   - **D.** a request from cooks for a fast cooking method

2. **Which most nearly describes the meaning of the word *colleague* as used in the passage?**
   - **A.** coworker
   - **B.** relative
   - **C.** student
   - **D.** friend

3. **Which of the following is true about the earliest microwave oven?**
   - **A.** It was immediately popular.
   - **B.** It caused radiation poisoning.
   - **C.** It was built in 1975.
   - **D.** It was big and heavy.

4. **What is most likely the purpose of the fifth paragraph?**
   - **A.** to point out that people didn't accept microwave ovens right away
   - **B.** to point out the early dangers of microwave cooking
   - **C.** to point out the superiority of gas ranges and ovens
   - **D.** to point out that smaller microwaves were the most popular kind

5. **Based on the passage, which of the following is the main reason for the popularity of microwave ovens?**
   - **A.** They move molecules fast.
   - **B.** They cook snacks.
   - **C.** They cook things quickly.
   - **D.** They have become cheap.

6. *Answer the following question using complete sentences:*
   The last paragraph states that cooking habits of Americans were "changed forever." How were they changed? Explain your answer in your own words.

Mary Edwards Walker

MARY EDWARDS WALKER certainly did not follow the path of most women who lived in America in the 1800s. For one thing, she went to medical school and became a doctor—a very rare accomplishment for women of the time. In addition, she was the first woman ever awarded the Congressional Medal of Honor, which the highest military honor the U.S. gives. This medal is awarded for extreme bravery during wartime. The first one was handed out during the Civil War. Mrs. Walker is still the only female to receive this highly prized medal. In fact, since the first one was awarded, only about 3,500 people have been awarded the Congressional Medal of Honor.

How did someone who was not a soldier earn a medal for bravery? Walker volunteered to work as a doctor with the Union Army when the Civil War broke out. However, the army didn't have any female surgeons, so she was only allowed to be a nurse. Later, Walker went to the front lines and began actually working as a surgeon, though she did so without pay. In 1863, she finally did receive a contract to work as a civilian assistant surgeon, making her the first official female U.S. Army Surgeon.

Walker often wore two pistols and rode a horse alone into enemy territory to treat civilians on both the Union and Confederate side, but at one point, she was captured by Confederate troops and charged with being a spy. She was sent to prison, but was released as part of a prisoner exchange after a few months.

After the war, Walker became a spokesperson for equal rights for women. She thought women's clothing styles were ridiculous and **restrictive**. How could a woman be truly free wearing tight-fitting undergarments, layers of petticoats, hats, and long, heavy dresses? Walker soon turned to dressing completely in men's clothing, even wearing a tall top hat on her head. She was arrested several times for "impersonating a man." Walker frequently spoke out for equality of the sexes in speeches that she delivered and in both of the books she wrote.

Throughout her adult life, Walker worked hard for the passage of the 19th Amendment, which would allow women to vote. Sadly, though, she died in 1919, less than a year before the Constitution was changed to give women the same voting rights as men have.

It would have made her happy, however, to know that she was buried in the black suit she wore most of her life. ●

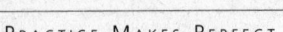

QUESTIONS

1. **Which statement best explains Mary Edwards Walker's importance in history?**
    - **A.** She graduated from medical school at a time when few women did.
    - **B.** She wore men's clothing and was arrested for "impersonating a man."
    - **C.** She helped many wounded civilians survive during the Civil War.
    - **D.** She was the first and only woman to receive the Congressional Medal of Honor.

2. **Which most nearly describes the meaning of the word _restrictive_ as used in the passage?**
    - **A.** anti-religious or immoral
    - **B.** limiting or confining
    - **C.** fashionable or trendy
    - **D.** elegant or dignified

3. **Which of the following can be inferred from the passage?**
    - **A.** Men of the time preferred that women stay in their traditional roles.
    - **B.** Few women of the time had what was needed to become a doctor.
    - **C.** The Civil War caused a great deal of hardship in America.
    - **D.** Most Americans supported the passage of the 19th Amendment.

4. **Based on information in the passage, which of the following statements is _not_ true about Walker?**
    - **A.** She sometimes carried two pistols with her.
    - **B.** She often wore a top hat and other men's clothing.
    - **C.** She thought women should have voting rights.
    - **D.** She worked only for the Union side in the Civil War.

5. **Walker refused to wear women's clothing, despite the problems she had when she wore men's clothing. Which of the following conclusions can you infer from this behavior?**
    - **A.** She chose to break the law in order to make people more open.
    - **B.** She did not respect anyone who dressed differently than she did.
    - **C.** She was willing to stand up, or even be arrested, for what she believed.
    - **D.** She did not care about those who disagreed with her ideas.

6. _Answer the following question using complete sentences:_
   At first, Walker was not allowed to work as a surgeon on the battlefield. Why do you think that changed? Explain in your own words.

What Smells?

IT HAPPENED OVER 40 years ago during recess at a country school, but everyone who was there still remembers it. Two brothers, Fritzi and Freddy, decided to hide inside an empty trash barrel. Unfortunately, when they crawled inside, they were met by an animal that had already claimed the space as its own—a skunk.

Fritzi and Freddy received a full blast of skunk spray—one of the most powerful and terrible odors known. Some have described the smell as something like a combination of garlic, rotten eggs, and burnt rubber. Even bears will back away from a skunk.

The brothers weren't the only ones to suffer after they met the skunk. Soon, everyone in the school was feeling sick from the smell. The boys were sent home, where their mother buried their clothes and scrubbed the boys with tomato juice, hoping for relief.

The boys probably would have been safe if they hadn't met up with the skunk in such a confined space. Skunks don't want to spray animals or people because they store a limited supply of their oil for protection, and it takes 10 days or so for their bodies to create more.

When a skunk encounters someone or something it **perceives** as dangerous, it often stomps its feet or lifts its tail, as if to say, "Hey! Do you see that I'm a *skunk*? You'd better get away from me." One type of skunk, the spotted skunk, sometimes even does a hand stand, trying to make itself look bigger to frighten away predators.

If nothing else works, and the skunk thinks its life might be in danger, it aims at the eyes of the enemy and releases a spray from glands underneath its tail. It can hit a target 6-10 feet away, but the odor can stretch for over a mile. The spray itself is oily, and small dogs have been known to die from it. The spray can coat their lungs and make breathing impossible and can also cause temporary blindness.

For most animals and humans, the spray isn't fatal—just disgusting. It's hard to get rid of, too. Many believe that soaking in tomato juice or beer will do the trick, but studies suggest that neither treatment really works. What does help, according to chemists, is a mixture of hydrogen peroxide, soap, and baking soda—as well as time. The smell eventually *does* go away, but it may take days. ●

QUESTIONS

1. **Which of the following is most likely the author's reason for including the story about Fritzi and Freddy?**
   A. to show how silly the boys were for hiding in a trash barrel
   B. to give a real-life example of how skunk spray can affect people
   C. to explain that skunks always try to warn their victims
   D. to show that tomato juice is not effective against skunk odor

2. **Which of the following is true about skunks?**
   A. They try to avoid spraying, when possible.
   B. The odor from skunk spray lasts a few hours.
   C. Their spray comes from glands located in their mouth.
   D. The odor can be smelled over five miles away.

3. **Which describes how the students at Fritzi and Freddy's school reacted after they were sprayed?**
   A. They laughed a lot.
   B. They went home.
   C. They ignored the smell.
   D. They got sick from the smell.

4. **As used in the passage, the word _perceives_ most nearly means**
   A. dislikes intensely.
   B. believes to be.
   C. takes aim at.
   D. protects fiercely.

5. **Skunks have distinctive black and white markings. Why do you think the author never mentions them?**
   A. The markings are different on every skunk.
   B. The focus of the passage is on a skunk's odor.
   C. The author simply did not mention the markings.
   D. Everyone already knows what a skunk looks like.

6. *Answer the following question using complete sentences:*
   Based on the passage, what do you think is the best action for a person to take if encountering a skunk? Explain in your own words.

Baths—A Comparison

MOST PEOPLE THINK that older civilizations had a primitive existence, even more so than people from more modern times had. That assumption is not always valid, though. Compare, for example, the lives of the colonists in early America with the lives of the ancient Romans, who lived in the 2nd century BCE. When it comes to a very basic part of life, personal cleanliness, the Romans were superior.

The fact is that people in Colonial America probably smelled terrible. Getting clean in the 1600s and 1700s meant sponging off with a damp cloth. Take a bath or shower? That was something few people did more than a couple of times a year.

There is a good reason baths were rare: They were a tremendous amount of work. Soap had to be made by hand, and a wooden tub had to be lugged into the house. Buckets of water had to be fetched from a well, heated on a stove, and then carried to the tub, which was usually in a bedroom. Homes did not have bathrooms, so privacy was also an issue. Homes, heated only by a stove, could be freezing cold in the winter, and the idea of taking a bath in the bedroom was not appealing to the general population. Furthermore, most people believed that bathing would take away natural oils and leave a person **vulnerable** to disease.

In wealthier families, clothes would be fresher than their owners' bodies. Servants would lay out clean shirts for the men each day and clean undergarments called "shifts" for the women. A wealthy man might own as many as 50 shirts. The clean shirts and shifts protected outer garments somewhat from body oils and perspiration.

In ancient Rome, things were a lot different. Both men and women typically took a bath every day at public baths, which were beautiful buildings full of pools fed by wooden or earthenware pipes. There were three kinds of pools—the tepidarium of warm water, the caldarium of hot water warmed with an underground heating system, and the frigidarium of cold water. The baths were quite luxurious, with saunas, exercise rooms, towels, and slaves to wait on people. Vendors even sold food.

The average ancient Roman was undoubtedly a lot cleaner than the average colonist was in early America, disproving the notion that life has constantly improved throughout the ages. ●

QUESTIONS

1. **Which of the following best states the purpose of the comparison made in the passage?**
   A. to show that ancient Romans were smarter than American colonists were
   B. to show that modern life is not always superior to life in ancient times
   C. to describe the three kinds of pools typically included in Roman baths
   D. to tell why baths were not taken frequently by the colonists in early America

2. **Which most nearly describes the meaning of the word *vulnerable* a used in the passage?**
   A. defenseless against; exposed
   B. dried out; without moisture
   C. frigid; frozen solid
   D. untreatable; often fatal

3. **Based on the passage, which of the following conclusions would be accurate?**
   A. Most Romans probably approved of slavery.
   B. Americans probably didn't care about a sense of smell.
   C. Americans were proud of being part of a community; Romans were not.
   D. Romans had running water, but American colonists did not.

4. **Based on the passage, which is *not* true about ancient Romans?**
   A. They placed a high value on personal cleanliness.
   B. They wanted their baths to be plain but efficient.
   C. They used slaves to help operate the baths.
   D. Both men and woman went to the baths daily.

5. **Which statement best reflects the purpose of the third paragraph?**
   A. to describe Colonial bedrooms and bathrooms
   B. to show how much work went into preparing a bath
   C. to show how much disease was caused by lack of cleanliness
   D. to show that wealthy people were cleaner than poor people were

6. *Answer the following question using complete sentences:*
   Summarize the primary difference between personal cleanliness in Colonial times and in Roman times, according to the facts in the article.

A Deadly Disease

On MAY 8, 1979, the World Health Organization announced that smallpox, the deadly disease that had killed millions of people throughout history, had been **eradicated**. No cases of the disease had been reported anywhere since 1977.

That announcement marked the end of suffering from one of the world's most feared plagues. The earliest evidence of smallpox was discovered in the mummified remains of the Egyptian pharaoh Ramses V, who died around 1156 BCE. There have also been frequent smallpox outbreaks over the years in many areas of the world, including Europe, Asia, and Africa. In addition, European settlers who had smallpox brought the disease to America, where it killed huge numbers of Native Americans.

People who contract smallpox usually suffer from flu-like symptoms, including headaches, backaches, and fever. After that, they develop sores in their mouths and a red rash, primarily on the face, arms, and legs. The rash then turns into horrible, pus-filled blisters. The disease was particularly hard on children, killing as many as 80% of those who were infected. The children who survived smallpox were often disfigured from scars left by the blisters, and many were left blind.

In 1796, a British doctor named Edward Jenner heard that milkmaids who had caught a mild disease called cowpox never came down with smallpox. He decided to test the theory. He took pus from a cowpox blister and inserted it into a small cut on an eight-year-old boy's arm. The boy became mildly ill. When the child recovered, Jenner repeated the process with a tiny bit of the real smallpox germs. The boy never contracted the disease, and Jenner was able to prove that this type of "vaccination" prevented smallpox. Experimenting on a small child seems shocking to us today, but what shocked people then was the idea of injecting anything from a cow into a human being. Jenner was widely ridiculed, and a cartoon of the time showed vaccinated people with cows coming out of their heads. Eventually, however, people saw the effectiveness of his method, and the death rate from smallpox plunged.

In 1967, the World Health Organization began a campaign to completely put an end to the disease. Whenever there was an outbreak anywhere, everyone in the vicinity would be vaccinated. Eventually, the efforts paid off, and the world is now free of smallpox, one of the deadliest diseases in recorded history. ◉

QUESTIONS

1. **According to the passage, which statement is true?**
   A. Cowpox can cause smallpox outbreaks.
   B. Cowpox proved that smallpox could be cured.
   C. Cowpox is less serious than smallpox is.
   D. Cowpox is a disease present in cows, not in humans.

2. **As used in the passage, the word *eradicated* most nearly means**
   A. eliminated.
   B. spread.
   C. vaccinated.
   D. discovered.

3. **Based on the information in the passage, which of the following is *not* a symptom of smallpox?**
   A. a red rash on the face
   B. headaches and backaches
   C. pus-filled blisters
   D. shortness of breath

4. **If people survived smallpox, they were likely to have which of the following?**
   A. scars on their face
   B. a crooked spine
   C. a loss of hearing
   D. mental problems

5. **Which of the following best states the purpose of the fourth paragraph?**
   A. to criticize Edward Jenner's methods of experimentation
   B. to explain how the smallpox vaccine was developed
   C. to describe smallpox outbreaks throughout history
   D. to tell how smallpox was eradicated around the world

6. *Answer the following question using complete sentences:*
   Do you think that Edward Jenner was justified in experimenting on a small child? Why or why not?

Black Holes

Black holes may be the strangest objects in the universe. Scientists believe they exist, but nobody has ever seen one. Even their name is strange since black holes aren't "holes" at all.

So what are they? That's not easy to explain. Imagine holding a kitchen sponge in one hand. Now, imagine squeezing that sponge in your hand until it is much, much smaller. The entire sponge still exists, but it is occupying a much smaller space than it did before.

Now imagine that you could keep squeezing that sponge until it is so small that it is invisible to the eye. What you would have then is something a bit similar to a black hole.

Black holes are created when a large star runs out of fuel and starts to shrink. Soon it collapses into itself, pulling surrounding objects with it. It's as if the star and anything close to it is squeezed, becoming smaller and smaller, until it cannot shrink any further. But, that object is so **dense** and has such a strong gravitational pull that nothing can escape from it, not even light, and yet, it keeps on pulling objects from space into it. Because no light can escape, no one can see it. That's why it is called a "black" hole. However, it isn't really a hole at all, and it isn't empty like a real "hole" on Earth is. It is out in space and actually exists, but because nothing can escape for astronomers to see in their telescopes, it is invisible.

If black holes are invisible, how do scientists know they exist? One way is by looking at objects in space that are behaving in an unusual way. For example, an object may be wobbling because something with a very strong gravitational pull—a black hole—is pulling it off course. The scientists can't see that black hole, but the behavior of objects around it shows that it is there.

Another way astronomers "see" a black hole is that there is a dark spot in an area of the sky that blocks out the stars that should be there. The "empty spot" frequently means that a black hole occupies that part of space.

Our sun is a star. Could it become a black hole and suck the earth into it? No. Luckily for us, only stars that are much larger than the sun become black holes. There are billions of black holes in space—in fact, our Milky Way has a huge black hole at its center. Our sun, though, won't ever become one of them. ●

QUESTIONS

1. **Why does the author have readers imagine squeezing a sponge?**
   A. The author wants to show how sponges and black holes are made up of similar material.
   B. The author wants to help explain what happens when something collapses into something smaller.
   C. The author wants to illustrate what happens when light cannot escape from an object.
   D. The author wants to show that anything can become a black hole, in the right circumstances.

2. **Which of the following is _not_ true about black holes?**
   A. They are invisible.
   B. They are incredibly dense.
   C. They are made from collapsing stars.
   D. They expand and contract.

3. **Which most nearly describes the meaning of the word _dense_ as used in the passage?**
   A. stupid
   B. compact
   C. light
   D. dark

4. **Which of the following best states the author's purpose?**
   A. to explain the difficult subject of black holes in simple language
   B. to point out that it is really impossible to understand black holes
   C. to show the positive effects black holes have on the universe
   D. to show the problems in the universe caused by black holes

5. **Which best describes one way scientists know black holes exist, even though these objects are invisible?**
   A. They detect them by enlarging photographs taken by telescopes.
   B. The odd behavior of some objects in space shows that a black hole may be near.
   C. Nearby objects reflect light from the black hole and show its location.
   D. Sometimes, objects fall into a black hole and emerge on the other side.

6. _Answer the following question using complete sentences:_
   The passage explains that a black hole is not really a "hole" at all. Why do you think the term "hole" is part of the name?

"Turtle" Goes to War

MOST PEOPLE THINK that the submarine is a fairly recent invention, something invented in the last 100 years or so. People who believe that, however, are wrong.

Submarines have been around for a *long* time. In fact, the first primitive submarine was actually built around 1620 by a Dutch inventor. A more advanced kind was built by a college student named David Bushnell in the early 1770s, and it became the first submarine ever used in warfare.

The one-man submarine was nicknamed "Turtle" because Bushnell thought it looked like two turtle shells joined together. It was only about nine feet long and made of wood strengthened with metal. The person closed inside Turtle had enough air for only about half an hour. He could make the submarine move with propellers that he operated with pedals like those on bicycles. His top speed, though, was only about three miles per hour. That speed is even slower than most people generally walk, which is about five miles per hour.

Bushnell also had other talents. He experimented with explosives and was the first to show that gunpowder could be exploded under water. In 1776, during the Revolutionary War, he worked with army officers to put both his explosives and Turtle to use. They intended to sink a British ship in New York harbor.

The plan was to tow Turtle as close as possible to the ship. The operator would then go underwater, approach the ship, and attach a mine. The plan worked—except that when the operator tried to attach the mine to the ship, he hit a metal **impediment** of some kind and could not attach the explosive. Two later attempts also failed because of tides and other issues, and a third was planned. However, the British sank the ship carrying Turtle before that could happen. Turtle was retrieved, but no one knows what eventually became of the submarine.

George Washington called Turtle's attempted attack an "effort of genius." Even though it didn't succeed in its mission, Turtle was an amazing creation that paved the way for the development of modern submarines, including their use in the Civil War, WWI, and WWII. ●

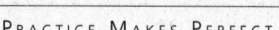

QUESTIONS

1. Which of the following best states the author's purpose?

   A. to show that submarines are extremely valuable during wartime

   B. to point out that submarines were invented more than 100 years ago

   C. to give information about the first submarine ever used in war

   D. to point out the intelligence of inventor David Bushnell

2. According to the passage, which statement is true about Turtle?

   A. It was named "Turtle" because it moved at only three miles per hour.

   B. It was unsuccessful in its attempt to sink a British ship.

   C. It was used in the Civil War.

   D. It was built by a Dutch inventor.

3. As used in the passage, *impediment* most nearly means

   A. a blockage.

   B. a hook.

   C. a gun.

   D. a huge wave.

4. Which statement below is *not* true about Turtle?

   A. Turtle was a one-man submarine.

   B. George Washington tried to use Turtle to attack a British ship.

   C. Turtle was the first submarine ever invented.

   D. Turtle was made of wood and metal.

5. How did the person operating Turtle survive underwater?

   A. He held his breath.

   B. A breathing tube led from Turtle to the surface of the water.

   C. Turtle held a small amount of air.

   D. A tank for providing air was operated with a pedal.

6. *Answer the following question using complete sentences:*
   Explain what Turtle was and why it was important.

A Very Strange Musical Instrument

IF YOU ARE LIKE most people, you have never seen a strange electronic musical instrument called the *theremin*. However, there is a good chance you have heard one. The eerie sound of the theremin has been used in many science fiction movies throughout the years and by rock bands such as Led Zeppelin and the Rolling Stones.

What makes the theremin unusual? Its appearance is like no other musical instrument. It consists of a box with two **protruding** antennas, one vertical and one horizontal. That's it. There are no strings, keys, levers, reeds, or other items usually associated with musical instruments.

After all, a modern piano has over 10,000 different parts and uses keys that force padded hammers to hit strings in order to make sounds. An electric guitar is usually held and played by hand. You have to blow into a clarinet or trumpet, and a drummer pounds his or her drums with wooden sticks or a foot pedal. This is not so with the theramin, however.

The most unusual characteristic is that musicians never touch the theremin when they are playing it. They make sounds by moving their hands in the air between the two antennas. They move a hand closer to the vertical antenna to raise the pitch and toward the horizontal antenna to lower the volume. The sounds are made in the electromagnetic fields surrounding the antenna.

The theremin was invented in the Soviet Union in 1919 by a Russian scientist named Léon Theremin. He toured Europe and the United States, giving public recitals and playing to packed houses. He later moved to the U.S., but in 1938, he mysteriously disappeared while living in New York City. According to many sources, Theremin had been kidnapped by secret service agents from the Soviet Union and imprisoned in a Siberian labor camp. He was later released and sent to work on the development of spy technology for the Soviet Union.

The theremin is not a well-known instrument today, but it still has many fans, and its popularity is said to be growing again. It is not easy to learn, but people all over the world still work on mastering the instrument with the strangely beautiful sound. ●

QUESTIONS

1. **Which of the following best states the author's purpose?**
    A. to give information about a little-known musical instrument
    B. to discuss the importance of the theremin in movies
    C. to show how important the theremin was to spy technology
    D. to describe how the theremin is played

2. **According to the passage, what is the most unusual feature of the theremin?**
    A. It has a beautiful but eerie sound.
    B. Its inventor played the theremin all over the world.
    C. Rock bands have used it in their songs.
    D. A musician's hands don't touch the theremin when playing it.

3. **As used in the passage, the word *protruding* most nearly means**
    A. sticking out.
    B. whirling.
    C. flat.
    D. colorful.

4. **The theremin is best described as**
    A. a drum-like instrument.
    B. an electronic instrument.
    C. a stringed instrument.
    D. a wind instrument.

5. **Based on the information in the passage, which of the following does a theremin look like?**
    A. a large round bowl made of wood
    B. a violin that has only one string
    C. a drum without any drumsticks
    D. a box that uses electric wires

6. ***Answer the following question using complete sentences:***
    Which movie title below would be most likely to include theremin music? Explain why you feel your answer is correct.
    A. *Goofball, the Crazy Poodle*
    B. *Haunted Mansions of the Moon*
    C. *Portrait of a Skier*
    D. *A Paris Love Story*

The Amazing Tarahumara

IT TAKES MOST RUNNERS at least four and a half hours to complete a marathon, which is exactly 26.2 miles long. Marathons are pretty easy, though, compared to ultramarathons such as Colorado's 100-mile long Leadville Trail 100 race. This race takes place in the rugged terrain of the Rocky Mountains and starts out at an altitude of over 10,000 feet. Even visitors who aren't participating in the race often find themselves short of breath in the high mountain air.

The Tarahumara runners from Mexico are *not* among those who generally have problems breathing in low-oxygen conditions. In fact, Tarahumara runners often win these extremely long races. While many other runners cross the finish line looking as if they are ready to die, the Tarahumara often appear almost **invigorated**, laughing, talking, and showing little fatigue. To the horror of many health-conscious racers, Tarahumara runners have even been known to stop for a cigarette break or two along the 100-mile route. Furthermore, the Tarahumara don't wear expensive, high-tech running shoes for these events; instead, they prefer rugged homemade sandals made of rubber tires.

It isn't only the Tarahumara young people who show such a tremendous ability to run long distances. A 52-year-old Tarahumara runner named Victoriano Churro came in first one year in the Leadville race, and his 41-year-old teammate came in second.

Who are these super runners? They are natives of the Copper Canyon area of northwestern Mexico, a rugged plateau whose land is composed of deep gorges and canyons, where people live far from each other. The Tarahumara call themselves Rarámuri, which means "fleet foot" or "foot runner." As children, they play running games, such as one that involves kicking a small wooden ball for distances of 50 to 100 miles or more, continuing for hours or even days without rest. When they get a little older, they also run great distances from settlement to settlement on narrow footpaths through canyons, just to communicate with one another. They have even been known to capture deer and mountain goats by running the wild animals to exhaustion.

People who have spent time with the Tarahumara often speak of the sheer joy the people take in running. Perhaps that is the main reason they have gained the reputation as the world's greatest long-distance runners. ●

QUESTIONS

1. **Which statement best reflects the author's likely purpose in opening the passage with information about marathons and ultramarathons?**
   - **A.** The author wants to promote the Leadville 100 to those who may not know about it.
   - **B.** The author wants to point out the difficulty of running at high altitudes.
   - **C.** The author wants to begin by impressing readers with what the Tarahumara can do.
   - **D.** The author wants to compare and contrast marathons with ultramarathons.

2. **As used in the passage, the word *invigorated* most nearly means**
   - **A.** delirious.
   - **B.** exhausted.
   - **C.** hysterical.
   - **D.** energized.

3. **Which of the following can be inferred about the Tarahumara?**
   - **A.** They have strong communities that help each other.
   - **B.** Young and old people run throughout most of their lives.
   - **C.** They would buy expensive sneakers if they could.
   - **D.** Most of them have moved to Leadville, Colorado.

4. **Which of the following is *not* true of the Tarahumara?**
   - **A.** They call themselves Rarámuri.
   - **B.** They run in shoes made of tires.
   - **C.** They usually live to a very old age.
   - **D.** They live in northwestern Mexico.

5. **Based on the passage, which of the following is a conclusion that might be made about the Leadville 100?**
   - **A.** Most observers have difficulty breathing.
   - **B.** It is a very long and difficult race to win.
   - **C.** Both men and women can race in it.
   - **D.** The Tarahumara usually win the race.

6. *Answer the following question using complete sentences:*
   Why do you think the Tarahumara place so much importance on running?

A Great Idea

IN 1937, A MAN named Chester Carlson had a great idea, an amazing and simple idea. The problem was that no one else thought his idea was great. He contacted some of the best-known companies in America about it, but they all turned him down.

Luckily, Carlson was not a man to give up easily, and he kept struggling to find backers to help him improve and market his invention. It took him over ten years, but a company finally took notice. That company was the one that eventually became known as the Xerox Corporation.

What was Chester Carlson's great idea? He created the process that became known as xerography—in other words, what is known as photocopying. His idea revolutionized the business world and made him an extremely wealthy man.

Carlson first came up with his idea while working in a patent office. He spent long hours making copies of documents by rewriting them by hand. His hand started cramping, so he put his creativity to work. He had been inventing things since he was 15. For example, he had drawn designs for a machine that cleaned shoes. This time, Carlson put is mind to work on a way to make copying documents easier. After much research and experimentation, he came up with the process that became the basis for photocopying.

The first photocopy machine was not a success, though. It was so hard to operate that a skilled operator had to go through 48 steps to create just one copy. Another ten years went by before a usable office photocopier was finally created. It was a huge hit, and soon Carlson was earning millions of dollars in royalties from his invention.

Though he was a millionaire many times over, Carlson didn't **flaunt** his wealth. He and his wife never moved from their original home. He quietly gave away almost 100 million dollars to schools, libraries, international relief agencies, organizations that promoted world peace, and many other worthy causes. He reportedly told his wife that his ambition was "to die a poor man."

At Carlson's funeral in 1968, the former secretary-general of the United Nations said, "To know Chester Carlson was to like him, to love him and to respect him…He belonged to that rare breed of leaders who generate in our hearts faith in man and hope for the future." ●

QUESTIONS

1. **Which of the following happened first?**
   A. A photocopy machine was built that was very hard to operate.
   B. Carlson invented a process that became the basis for xerography.
   C. Carlson drew up plans for a machine that could clean shoes.
   D. Carlson gave away millions of dollars to worthy causes.

2. **Which most nearly describes the meaning of the word *flaunt* as used in the passage?**
   A. display
   B. earn
   C. correct
   D. conceal

3. **Based on the facts in the passage, which statement is true?**
   A. The first photocopy machine made Carlson much more money than the second.
   B. The second photocopy machine was much bigger than the first.
   C. The second photocopy machine was not nearly as popular as the first.
   D. The first photocopy machine was much harder to use than the second.

4. **Based on the passage, what characteristic do you think the author most admires about Carlson?**
   A. his scientific mind
   B. his generosity toward others
   C. his love and respect for his wife
   D. his sharp intelligence

5. **Which of the following does *not* seem to be one of Chester Carlson's qualities?**
   A. persistence
   B. kindness
   C. creativity
   D. selfishness

6. *Answer the following question using complete sentences:*
   Based on the facts given in the article, what type of man do you think Carlson was?

Ötzi the Iceman

IMAGINE HIKING IN the mountains, and you see a body. That's what happened in 1991 to two hikers who had decided to take a shortcut in the Alps. They were horrified, believing they had discovered a hiker who had become lost and died. They took pictures and reported it to authorities.

Was it a lost hiker? Authorities thought it was possibly a murder. The next day, a policeman and another person tried to **extract** the body, which was frozen in ice up to its torso. They used drills and ice axes, but they didn't have much luck. The weather worsened, and they had to abandon the task. A few days later, the body was finally retrieved and taken to the University of Innsbruck in Austria. Scientists determined that it was not a body from recent times. However, they didn't know how old the body actually was.

After some analysis, scientists determined that the body was the mummy of a man who lived over 5,300 years ago. He has become known as Ötzi, the Iceman. ("Ötzi" comes from the name of the Ötz Valley, near where the body was discovered.)

Ötzi was a small man by today's standards—only about 5'2" tall and 110 pounds. He was wearing a fur robe and cap, a woven grass cape, and shoes made of leather and stuffed with grass. He carried an ax, a dagger, a bow, a quiver of arrows, and a leather pouch. He also carried a wooden frame that probably served as a backpack for carrying supplies. Although he was only about 25-35 years old, Ötzi had already suffered from broken ribs, a broken nose, arthritis, and an intestinal parasite called whipworm. In addition, Ötzi had mysterious markings that may have been an early form of tattoo or the markings of a treatment for illness. We will never know for sure.

How did Ötzi die? An arrow in his shoulder and wounds on his hands and head suggest that he had been in a fight in the mountains and bled to death. Then, a glacier covered Ötzi's remains and preserved them until they were discovered thousands of years later.

The remarkable state of his body has allowed scientists to learn a great deal about humans who lived long ago. In fact, in 2012, scientists announced that the Iceman had suffered from Lyme disease and had brown eyes. They also recovered some red blood cells, making Ötzi's the oldest specimen of blood ever collected. ●

QUESTIONS

1. **Which of the following best describes the author's purpose?**
   - **A.** to show the places ancient people traveled
   - **B.** to explain how ancient people lived and fought
   - **C.** to give information about the discovery of an ancient man
   - **D.** to describe how the Iceman was dressed when he died

2. **Which statement is *not* true, based on what is known about Ötzi?**
   - **A.** Ötzi carried supplies in a backpack.
   - **B.** Ötzi probably had children.
   - **C.** Ötzi was shot with an arrow.
   - **D.** Ötzi had diseases and injuries.

3. **As used in the passage, what does *extract* most nearly mean?**
   - **A.** cover
   - **B.** shake
   - **C.** thaw
   - **D.** remove

4. **Based on the passage, which of the following statements is true?**
   - **A.** Ötzi was thought to have been a lost hiker.
   - **B.** Ötzi was murdered by a neighboring tribe.
   - **C.** Ötzi was very old when he died.
   - **D.** Ötzi was probably a shepherd.

5. **Which of the following describes Ötzi's appearance?**
   - **A.** He wore clothing made of natural materials.
   - **B.** He wore a fur-lined pair of pants.
   - **C.** He wore a hat made of grasses and straw.
   - **D.** He carried a pouch woven from linen.

6. *Answer the following question using complete sentences:*
   Based on the information in the article, why do you think scientists would have been interested in studying Ötzi the Iceman?

Brrrrrr!

Suppose that you were going on vacation and could choose to stay in any hotel in the world. Would you choose a luxurious penthouse? A cozy cottage tucked away in the mountains? A tropical island paradise surrounded by palm trees and ocean views?

Or, would you be one of the growing number of people who choose an ice hotel? That's right, a hotel made entirely of ice. Your bedroom would have a temperature of only 17-23°F—well below freezing. You would sleep on a slab of ice. Such lodgings aren't for everyone, but many travelers are attracted to the unique experience of staying in an ice hotel.

The first ice hotel came about almost by accident. The town of Jukkasjärvi, Sweden, located 124 miles north of the Arctic Circle, is busy in the summer with nature hikes and whitewater rafting trips for tourists. However, in the summer of 1990, the town built an igloo to hold a temporary art exhibit. (*Igloo* is the Inuit, or Eskimo, word for "snow house.")

The art exhibit attracted so many tourists that the town ran out of places for them to sleep. Some people decided to sleep in the igloo on reindeer hides. Afterwards, they raved about their unusual experience, and an idea was born.

Now, a new IceHotel is built every year in Jukkasjärvi, and people come from all over the world to stay in the rooms. Everything inside of the hotel is made of ice also, including the tables, chairs, and beds. Even the glasses in the bar are made of ice. Guests sleep in sleeping bags on top of mattresses and reindeer hides. Luckily, the bathrooms are in a separate building that is heated.

Since IceHotel was created, other ice hotels have been built in Norway, Finland, Sweden, Canada, and Romania. Each year, the hotels melt in the spring, and new hotels are constructed in the winter. The hotels generally take five to six weeks to build and use thousands of tons of ice. The blocks of ice are held together with *snice*, which is a kind of frozen water that looks like snow, but has the properties of ice.

Ice hotels are sometimes called **extravagant** igloos, with beautiful rooms, colored lights, and ice sculptures on ice pedestals. Guests often describe a feeling of accomplishment after spending a night there. They also describe the hotels as glittering, magical, and, well, cold! ○

QUESTIONS

1. **Which of the following best describes the author's purpose?**
   - **A.** to poke fun at people who stay in ice hotels
   - **B.** to give details about the substance called snice
   - **C.** to tell where ice hotels are located
   - **D.** to give basic information about ice hotels

2. **Which of the following best describes the purpose of the third paragraph?**
   - **A.** to compare ice hotels to igloos made by Inuits
   - **B.** to explain how ice hotels began
   - **C.** to promote tourism in Sweden
   - **D.** to explain what an igloo is

3. **As used in the last paragraph, the word *extravagant* most nearly means**
   - **A.** luxurious.
   - **B.** chilly.
   - **C.** temporary.
   - **D.** sparkling.

4. **Based on the article, which statement is true about Jukkasjärvi, Sweden?**
   - **A.** It has a large population.
   - **B.** It attracts tourists.
   - **C.** It has a strong Inuit culture.
   - **D.** It gets more snow than most other cities do.

5. **Based on the article, which statement is *not* true of ice hotels?**
   - **A.** The bedrooms include thick down comforters.
   - **B.** The beds are made from slabs of ice.
   - **C.** The ice bricks are held together with snice.
   - **D.** The hotels melt every spring.

6. ***Answer the following question using complete sentences:***
   If you had the chance, would you stay in an ice hotel? In your response, list the advantages and disadvantages of ice hotels.

Navajo Code Talkers

AFTER WORLD WAR II began for the United States, American military forces were faced with a problem that might lose the war for them if they couldn't solve it. They needed to communicate between locations in coded radio messages, but Japanese intelligence experts kept breaking the codes. No matter how complicated the Americans made the codes, the Japanese were able to **decipher** their messages.

A man named Phillip Johnston heard about the problem and had a brilliant idea. Because he had grown up on a Navajo reservation as the son of a missionary, he spoke the Navajo language—one of only about 30 non-native speakers in the world. At the time, the language had no written form at all, and Johnston thought it might be used as a basis for messages, using Navajo speakers.

With the permission of top commanders, he recruited 29 Navajo men and boys, some as young as 15, and they became the "Navajo Code Talkers." They gathered a list of Navajo words to describe various military terms. A submarine goes underwater, so they used the Navajo word for *fish* to mean *submarine*. They used the Navajo word for *potato* to mean *hand grenade* because the two objects look similar.

They also assigned a Navajo word to each letter of the English alphabet. The Navajo word for *ant* was used for "A." The Navajo word for bear was used for "B," etc. If a military commander wanted to send a message mentioning the direction of an attack, the Code Talkers might use the Navajo words for *nut, owl, rabbit, turkey,* and *horse* in a sentence: "Nesh-chee ne-ash-jsn gah than-zie lin." The initial letters of those words translated into English spell out *north*. This technique made the coded message nearly impossible to understand by the enemy.

The Code Talkers were sent to work with marines in the Pacific, but they were not allowed to write anything down in their language and had to remember every word precisely when they were in a battle situation. They became widely respected for this ability. In the important battle of Iwo Jima, they sent over 800 coded transmissions perfectly in the first 48 hours alone.

The Navajo Code Talkers played a vital role in helping win the war. Because of their efforts, the Japanese could no longer monitor radio communications on the battlefield. For the remaining years of the war, the Japanese never cracked the code used by the Code Talkers. ◗

QUESTIONS

1. **Which statement best describes the purpose of the first paragraph?**
    A. to explain the different sides involved in World War II
    B. to show how the Japanese cracked U.S. codes in World War II
    C. to tell about a problem the U.S. was having in World War II
    D. to detail how messages were intercepted in World War II

2. **As used in the passage, the word _decipher_ most nearly means**
    A. destroy any evidence.
    B. transcribe in writing.
    C. transmit over the air.
    D. figure out the meaning.

3. **Which of the following is a conclusion that might be drawn from the passage?**
    A. The Code Talkers enlisted at a young age.
    B. The Code Talkers had good memories.
    C. The Code Talkers didn't participate in combat.
    D. The Code Talkers understood many Japanese words.

4. **Which of the following statements is _not_ supported by the passage?**
    A. Phillip Johnston grew up on a reservation.
    B. Phillip Johnston learned to read Navajo at a reservation school.
    C. Phillip Johnston came up with the idea of using Navajo for codes.
    D. Phillip Johnston was the son of a missionary.

5. **Which statement best describes the most important outcome of the Code Talkers' work?**
    A. Intelligence experts learned that Navajos could contribute to the war effort.
    B. The Japanese were no longer able to decipher and disrupt radio communication.
    C. Phillip Johnston was able to recruit 29 Navajo men and boys for the military.
    D. The Navajo eventually developed an alphabet and a written form of communication.

6. _Answer the following question using complete sentences:_
    Why do you think the Code Talkers tried to describe military terms according to what those terms resembled?

From Hair to Millionaire

"I am a woman who came from the cotton fields of the South. From there I was promoted to the washtub. From there I was promoted to the cook kitchen. And from there I promoted myself into the business of manufacturing hair goods and preparations....I have built my own factory on my own ground."

MADAM C.J. WALKER, 1912

The person quoted above was a woman of remarkable accomplishments. Born in 1867 to former slaves, she was named Sarah Breedlove. Her parents died when she was only seven; she and an older sister survived by picking cotton. Sarah did not attend school because Louisiana did not provide funds for the education of black children at that time. She was only 14 when she married, but her husband died six years later, leaving her with a two-year-old daughter.

Later in life, in her thirties, Breedlove suffered from a scalp problem and lost some of her hair. Upset and embarrassed, she began experimenting with homemade remedies and developed her own recipes to stop hair loss and make her hair grow in faster.

In 1905, she married a man named Charles Joseph Walker, and from then on, she called herself Madam C.J. Walker. The two of them began traveling through the southern and eastern states, selling her "Wonderful Hair Grower" and other products door-to-door. At the time, there were very few items on the market specifically for black women, and her products became quite popular. She soon opened a beauty school and a factory, and in only 15 years, built the C.J. Walker Manufacturing Company into a highly successful business that employed over 3,000 people worldwide.

Madam Walker is generally recognized as the first African American woman to become a self-made millionaire, but she is also known as a **philanthropist** who used her wealth and influence to support many worthy causes. She helped fight for legislation to make lynching a federal crime, and she donated money to black schools, orphanages, retirement homes, and other charitable organizations throughout her life.

Madam Walker possessed a mind that was perfect for business, but she also worked at it. She once said, "There is no royal flower-strewn path to success. And if there is, I have not found it—for if I have accomplished anything in life it is because I have been willing to work hard." ●

QUESTIONS

1. **What is the most probable reason for including the quotation by Madam Walker at the beginning of the passage?**
   - A. to show that she was very generous with her money
   - B. to indicate that she once worked as a cook
   - C. to show how she got better jobs to take control of her future
   - D. to show the various promotions she received in her life

2. **According to the passage, Madam Walker would most likely agree with which of the following statements?**
   - A. Hair loss shouldn't be fixed.
   - B. Fourteen is not too young for marriage.
   - C. Education is not as important as luck.
   - D. Success comes from working hard.

3. **Which most nearly describes the meaning of the word *philanthropist* as used in the passage?**
   - A. a person who works to make lynching a federal crime
   - B. a person who gives generously to worthy causes
   - C. a person who is able to earn millions in a short time
   - D. a person who starts a business and makes it successful

4. **According to the article, which of the following terms would *not* be true of Madam Walker?**
   - A. She was a professor.
   - B. She was an important inventor.
   - C. She was a success in business.
   - D. She was a supporter of charities.

5. **Which of the following statements best describes the reason for the next-to-last paragraph?**
   - A. It explains that she was an African American businesswoman.
   - B. It explains that she worked hard to become a wealthy woman.
   - C. It explains that she used the money she made for good purposes.
   - D. It explains that she hated prejudice and worked to end it.

6. *Answer the following question using complete sentences:*
   In your own words, why do you think Madam Walker was interested in helping black schools and orphanages?

The Thrill of the Ride

SOME PEOPLE NEVER grow up. That could describe members of an organization called American Coaster Enthusiasts (ACE). While other adults might relax with activities such as playing golf, reading, gardening, or going to the movies, members of this organization meet all over the world to ride roller coasters.

ACE has over 5,000 members in 16 countries and publishes a bi-monthly newsletter. They work to preserve wooden roller coasters in danger of being torn down or in need of repair. Their efforts have helped rescue and **refurbish** the Giant Dipper in San Diego, California, and the oldest roller coaster in the world, Leap-the-Dips, located in Altoona, Pennsylvania.

Roller coasters have a long history. They originated in the 15th century in Russia as "Russian Mountains." People created ice-covered hills and built sleds of wood. Then they would climb stairs that were 70 or 80 feet high, reach the top of the ice-covered hill, get into a wooden sled, and head down. It was a short but very fast ride.

Some people say the first real roller coaster with wheels was built in 1784 in Saint Petersburg, Russia, under the orders of Catherine the Great. Others say it was built in Paris in 1804. A primitive form of roller coaster came to the United States in 1827, when a mining company built a track almost nine miles long to transport coal downhill to the town of Mauch Chunk, Pennsylvania. Soon people were paying fifty cents to enjoy a thrilling ride down the hill on the coal carts.

The first modern roller coaster was built on Coney Island in Brooklyn, New York, in 1884. Called the Gravity Switchback Railway, it was primitive by today's standards, but it was a hit with customers, even though they had to climb to the top of a platform to get into a car. For many years, roller coaster tracks were made of wooden railroad ties, but in 1959, Disneyland introduced the Matterhorn Bobsleds, which use a steel track. That was a breakthrough in the world of roller coasters because steel could be bent to allow loops, corkscrews, and other innovations. Now, roller coasters send riders on trips that no one could even have imagined in the early days of the ride.

Some of those riders are, of course, members of ACE, people who have never forgotten the thrill of their first trip on a roller coaster. ●

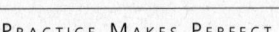

QUESTIONS

1. Which of the following statements is *not* true about what you just read?
   A. The passage gives a short history of the development of roller coasters.
   B. The passage tells about a group called American Coaster Enthusiasts.
   C. The passage mentions the development of bendable steel tracks.
   D. The passage describes what happens to a person when riding a roller coaster.

2. As used in the passage, the word *refurbish* most nearly means
   A. tear down.
   B. fix up.
   C. move away.
   D. write about.

3. Which of the following developments came first?
   A. the coal train to Mauch Chunk
   B. Matterhorn Bobsleds
   C. Russian Mountains
   D. Leap-the-Dips

4. Which of the following best describes the Gravity Switchback Railway, according to the article?
   A. It was the first modern roller coaster.
   B. It was built in St. Petersburg, Russia.
   C. People did not appreciate it at all.
   D. It was used to transport coal downhill.

5. Which statement best describes the reason for including the fifth paragraph?
   A. to give Disneyland credit for developing and building Matterhorn Bobsleds
   B. to explain what development made loops and other modern roller coaster features possible
   C. to explain why railroad ties are not used in modern roller coaster construction
   D. to point out that ACE helps protect endangered roller coasters around the world

6. *Answer the following question using complete sentences:*
   Why do you think roller coasters have remained popular over the years?

You Think You Have a Hard Life?

THE NEXT TIME YOU feel like complaining because you have to take out the trash, do your homework, or make your bed, be thankful that you did not live in ancient Sparta. Children born in this Greek city-state three thousand years ago had a rough life.

Babies born in Sparta were inspected carefully by officials, and those who seemed weak or unhealthy were taken to a hillside and left to die.

At age seven, boys were taken from their mothers to live together and train as soldiers. Older boys beat younger ones in order to toughen them up. The boys had little clothing and marched without shoes. They were also purposely underfed so that they would have to learn to steal food. Boys who were caught stealing food, however, were beaten—not for stealing, but for getting caught. It wasn't that the Spartans wanted the boys to be dishonest; the adults wanted them to be **shrewd** and learn survival skills. Boys were also taught that nothing was more disgraceful than surrendering in battle. They should win or die.

Children were told stories about strength and enduring pain bravely. One story was about a boy who caught a fox, intending to eat it. When he saw soldiers coming, he hid the fox under his shirt and let the animal eat his insides, rather than cry out in pain.

Spartan girls were also sent to school at age seven, though they probably lived at home. Physical training was emphasized, and the girls studied wrestling and gymnastics. They were also taught to fight and to participate in athletic events. The Spartans believed that physically strong mothers would produce physically strong children.

With its harsh training and discipline, Sparta created powerful armies that, for many years, were practically unbeatable in battle. The Spartans conquered many countries and enslaved the people, and the warrior state continued until it finally lost its power in 371 BC when Thebes, another Greek city-state, defeated it.

Today, the word *spartan* is used when referring to certain ways of life. When someone says that people had a "Spartan upbringing," for example, it means that they grew up with strict discipline and few luxuries.

Having to take out the trash, do your homework, or make your bed does *not* mean *you* have a Spartan existence! ◐

QUESTIONS

1. **Based on the passage, which statement most accurately describes the author's attitude toward young people today?**
   A. The author believes that children today should also be disciplined harshly.
   B. The author believes that children today have it easy compared to Spartan children.
   C. The author believes that girls today should get as much physical training as Spartan girls.
   D. The author admires the bravery of the Spartans, but thinks the harsh training was not worth it.

2. **Which most nearly describes the meaning of the word *shrewd* as used in the passage?**
   A. hungry; starving
   B. powerful; strong
   C. tricky; clever
   D. slow; plodding

3. **Which of the following would a young Spartan boy *not* experience?**
   A. hunger
   B. pain
   C. discipline
   D. encouragement

4. **Which statement most accurately describes the Spartan attitude toward girls?**
   A. They should not receive any education at all.
   B. They should study music, dancing, and literature.
   C. They should be trained to obey Spartan men.
   D. They should be trained to be physically strong.

5. **What is the most likely reason Spartans told children the story about the boy and the fox?**
   A. They wanted to show how a person who steals should not be punished.
   B. They wanted to emphasize the importance of protecting animals.
   C. They wanted to show how brave the boy was to endure pain without complaining.
   D. They wanted to prove the importance of being able to lie.

6. *Answer the following question using complete sentences:*
   Why do you think Spartans treated their children so harshly?

Dr. Seuss

IT'S A GOOD THING that the famous children's book author, Dr. Seuss, was a **persistent** man. Otherwise, children all over the world wouldn't have the pleasure of reading his delightful books, such as *Green Eggs and Ham*, *The Cat in the Hat*, and *How the Grinch Stole Christmas*! No one was interested in publishing his first book, *And to Think That I Saw It on Mulberry Street*. He submitted it to 29 publishers, and they all turned it down. But the author did not give up because he had just met an old classmate who had just been appointed editor of the juvenile section of a publishing company. He was interested in the book, and the rest is history.

Was Dr. Seuss really a doctor, though? No, he was a writer and a cartoonist, and his real name was Theodor Seuss Geisel. He began writing ads, and he became well known, because of his cartoons for an insect spray called Flit. One of his cartoons showed a ventriloquist holding a dummy, while a giant insect flew toward them. The dummy said, "Quick, Henry! The Flit!" That line became a popular phrase all over the country. In the face of just about any emergency or problem, people would say, "Quick, Henry! The Flit!"

Geisel continued to work in advertising for 30 years, but he wrote children's books on the side. After he had published his eleventh book, an editor suggested that Dr. Seuss write a primer for children learning to read. The editor told him to write a story that first graders can't put down, one that used no more than 346 different words. Dr. Seuss did— *The Cat in the Hat*, which used only 236 different words in its 72 pages. It was an immediate success. Another editor then challenged him to write a book that used 50 different words. That book became *Green Eggs and Ham*, his best-selling title ever. Many of his books continue to sell nearly 500,000 copies a year!

Geisel wrote and illustrated 44 books in his lifetime under the name Dr. Seuss. These books have sold over 222 million copies and have been translated into more than 15 languages. Although Dr. Seuss died in 1991, his books full of nonsensical rhymes, strange creatures, and great stories continue to delight both children and adults all over the world. ●

QUESTIONS

1. As used in the passage, the word *persistent* most nearly means
   A. selfish.
   B. brilliant.
   C. lazy.
   D. determined.

2. According to the passage, which of the following statements is true about Dr. Seuss?
   A. He started out his career as a writer of picture books for toddlers.
   B. He wrote *The Cat in the Hat* as the result of a suggestion from an editor.
   C. He wrote *Green Eggs and Ham* after eating some colored eggs.
   D. He became famous because he improved young children's reading skills.

3. Which of the following is true about the books Dr. Seuss wrote?
   A. The insecticide called Flit was often featured.
   B. He illustrated the books with his own cartoons.
   C. His best-selling book has always been *The Cat in the Hat*.
   D. His books were successful almost immediately.

4. Which best describes the purpose of the second paragraph?
   A. to explain how popular the insecticide Flit was in the 1920s and 1930s
   B. to explain that Dr. Seuss wasn't really a doctor of medicine at all
   C. to explain how Dr. Seuss chose the name that he was to use in all his writing
   D. to show that Dr. Seuss first used his cartooning ability in advertising

5. What is the main idea Dr. Seuss had in mind when writing *The Cat in the Hat*?
   A. to make as many rhymes as he could think of for "cat"
   B. to entertain children, even though he never had any of his own
   C. to experiment with using only 50 different words in a book
   D. to write a book that first graders wouldn't be able to put down

6. *Answer the following question using complete sentences:*
   The passage mentions two challenges editors gave to Dr. Seuss. What do you think his acceptance of those challenges indicates about him? Base your answers on information from the article and not just on your opinions.

How Words Get Into Dictionaries

Suppose that some people are looking at pictures of models, and they decide that some of the glamorous fashions are hideous. They start calling clothes they hate *glideous*. The term catches on, and soon many students in their school use *glideous*. Someone decides to look the word up in the dictionary, but it's not there. Does that mean that *glideous* isn't a word? No. It simply means that it is not used widely enough to make it into the dictionary.

People generally assume that a dictionary is a rule book, but most modern dictionaries are not. They simply try to describe language as it is really used. For example, you will find the word *ain't* in most dictionaries because it is something that people actually say. However, that doesn't mean that an English teacher will be happy to see the word show up in an assignment. Most dictionaries point out that the word is considered slang.

So, how are words put into the dictionary? Dictionary editors generally spend part of every day collecting examples of how words are used. In the past, they had to write down the references on slips of paper, but today, they enter the examples in huge online data bases. When a new word starts showing up in a wide variety of places, it is considered ready for inclusion in a dictionary.

The kind of dictionary that most of us use is called an **abridged** dictionary and includes only the most commonly used words. Editors have to make decisions about which words to include and which to leave out, and all dictionaries have different standards. That's why you might find a word listed in one dictionary, but not in another.

Another problem dictionaries have is that the English language changes so fast that it's hard to keep current. For example, the word *e-mail* started out with a hyphen in it, but when people started spelling the word *email*, some dictionaries changed to reflect that hyphen-less spelling. Texting didn't exist a few years ago, so older dictionaries will make no mention of it, but more current ones will.

The most comprehensive dictionary of English is the Oxford English Dictionary (OED); a recently printed edition is 22,000 pages long. The online edition, however, stays more current, with updates every three months. In fact, if *glideous* should suddenly catch on around the country, it would probably appear first in the online edition of the OED. ❂

QUESTIONS

1. **Which is the most likely reason that the author writes about the made-up word** *glideous*?
    A. to show that any term that people use is a word, even if they make it up themselves
    B. to explain why a dictionary would not include *glideous* in its list of terms
    C. to show that English teachers rely on dictionaries when grading student papers
    D. to explain how dictionaries set the rules for how words are used in English

2. **Which of the following is necessary for a word to appear in a dictionary?**
    A. The word must not be considered slang.
    B. The word must appear frequently in a variety of sources.
    C. The word must be easily understood by most people.
    D. The word must not include a hyphen in its spelling.

3. **Which most nearly describes the meaning of the word** *abridged* **as used in the passage?**
    A. full-length
    B. printed
    C. ordinary
    D. shortened

4. **Which statement is** *not* **a reason a word may appear in one dictionary and not in another?**
    A. Different dictionaries have different standards for what to include.
    B. Some dictionaries are printed before a word becomes widely used.
    C. An abridged dictionary can't include all words, so some have to be left out.
    D. Some editors aren't aware that a word has become popular across the country.

5. **Based on information in the passage, the OED can best be described as**
    A. a rarely updated dictionary.
    B. a long, in-depth dictionary.
    C. a dictionary that is popular in college.
    D. a dictionary used by English speakers.

6. *Answer the following question using complete sentences:*
   Why do you think some dictionaries include the word *ain't*, **and others do not, if teachers don't want students to use it? Base your answer on the facts in the article.**

Arsenic and the Victorians

LIVING IN GREAT BRITAIN during the Victorian Age had its drawbacks. One of them was the danger of arsenic poisoning. It wasn't that murderers were lurking around every corner ready to poison someone—the greatest danger came from everyday life.

Arsenic is a poisonous white powder that can cause terrible suffering and death, whether it is eaten, inhaled, or absorbed through the skin. Arsenic was kept in the kitchen of many Victorian homes to kill rats. Because it has no taste or odor, it was often mistaken for flour or sugar. In the first two years of Queen Victoria's rule, over 500 people died from accidentally **ingesting** arsenic. One poor woman accidentally used arsenic instead of sugar when making a dessert for her family, and she killed five of her nine children.

Arsenic was also used for other purposes, including medicine. Some doctors prescribed small quantities for pain. Thinking it could treat asthma, others had their patients smoke pipes containing tobacco mixed with arsenic. Charles Darwin took arsenic to treat his skin problem, probably contributing to the ill health he suffered through much of his life.

In the strangest use of this particular poison, many women of the time ate wafers made of chalk, vinegar, and arsenic, hoping to whiten their complexions. They also rubbed a mixture containing the same three substances on their skin to whiten it. Arsenic was definitely a deadly fashion.

Pale skin, though, wasn't the only dangerous fashion. Arsenic was used in dyes to create a shade of green, which became a hugely popular color in the nineteenth century. Women's clothes were often dyed with a product called "Scheele's green," which also dyed toys, flowers, candles, playing cards, wallpaper, and other products. Many arsenic poisonings resulted from simply sleeping in a bedroom with wallpaper dyed with Scheele's green. Although these people didn't usually die, they reported such symptoms as inflamed eyes, headaches, and sore throats— symptoms that went away when they would leave their homes for vacations or other trips.

Sadly, even when the dangers of arsenic became more and more well known, efforts to regulate its use failed. Companies made a lot of money putting arsenic in products, and it was many years before the health of the citizens became more important than the financial health of the companies who used arsenic. ●

QUESTIONS

1. **Which of the following best states the author's purpose?**
   A. to show how effective arsenic is as a murder weapon
   B. to show arsenic affected everyday life many years ago
   C. to show sympathy for the mother who accidentally poisoned her children
   D. to comment on the importance of environmental and personal safety

2. **As used in the passage, the word** *ingesting* **most nearly means**
   A. selling.
   B. inhaling.
   C. smelling.
   D. swallowing.

3. **From the passage, it can be inferred that the term "Victorian Age" refers to**
   A. the years that Great Britain was victorious in war.
   B. the years that Queen Victoria was Queen of England.
   C. a time when people were quite ignorant.
   D. the age when regulation of arsenic began.

4. **How was arsenic used to treat asthma?**
   A. It was rubbed on the skin.
   B. It was taken in wafer form.
   C. It was smoked in a pipe.
   D. It was eaten in desserts.

5. **After reading the passage, which can you say was** *not* **a use of arsenic in the Victorian Age?**
   A. to kill cockroaches
   B. to lighten complexions
   C. to kill rats
   D. to dye cloth

6. *Answer the following question using complete sentences:*
   Although the author does not discuss arsenic as a murder weapon, why do you think that it might have often been used by murderers? Base your answer on the facts in the article.

The Rock

THE FORMER maximum-security prison known as Alcatraz still sits on an island in San Francisco Bay. Today, the facility is a tourist attraction, but from 1934 to 1963, it served as a home for some of the most dangerous convicts in America. Men sentenced to serve time in Alcatraz had some good news and some bad news in store for them.

The good news: Prisoners didn't have to share a cell with anyone.

The bad news: The cells were so small that most inmates could stand in the middle and touch both walls.

The good news: Prisoners could have visitors.

The bad news: They could have only one visitor per month. That visitor had to be approved by the warden, and all talking was through an intercom, with no physical contact allowed.

The good news: The food was reportedly some of the best in the prison system at the time.

The bad news: The only time talking was allowed was during meals and recreation periods. Before this rule was suspended, prisoners went to desperate lengths to try to communicate with one another. A common technique was to empty the water in their toilets and use the sewage pipes as a primitive kind of communication system.

Not surprisingly, a number of prisoners tried to escape from Alcatraz over the years, but there is no evidence that any were successful. The most famous, though, were Frank Morris and the Anglin brothers, John and Clarence. They worked for years on their elaborate escape plans, stealing tools, digging a passageway through an air vent, building rubber rafts, making life preservers out of raincoats, and creating lifelike dummies to leave in their cells. On the night of June 11, 1962, they left the dummies in their beds, escaped through the vents, climbed onto the roof, and down to their rubber rafts. The escape was discovered the next morning, but they were never seen again.

What happened to them? No one knows; though prison officials conducted an extensive search, they were never found. Most authorities believe that all three men almost certainly drowned.

Alcatraz was the most expensive system in the country to operate, and the decision was made to close it in 1963. In 1972, the prison became part of Golden Gate National Park. ●

QUESTIONS

1. **What would be the best reason for the author's decision to describe both "good news" and" bad news" as they related to Alcatraz?**
    - **A.** to amuse readers and make them laugh
    - **B.** to describe what life was like for a prisoner there
    - **C.** to show how terrible prison life was
    - **D.** to show that life wasn't that bad for inmates

2. **As used in the passage, the word *elaborate* most nearly means**
    - **A.** illegal.
    - **B.** secret.
    - **C.** complicated.
    - **D.** simple.

3. **Which was *not* a part of the Frank Morris and Anglin brothers' escape plan?**
    - **A.** being hidden in a supply boat leaving the island
    - **B.** creating life preservers out of raincoats
    - **C.** hiding lifelike dummies in their beds at night
    - **D.** digging a passageway through an air vent

4. **What can you infer is the most likely reason criminals were sent to Alcatraz?**
    - **A.** Alcatraz was on the West coast, where most crime was committed at that time.
    - **B.** Its location on an island made it especially difficult for any escapees to make it to shore.
    - **C.** The idea was to keep the worst criminals together in one place, and Alcatraz was it.
    - **D.** The prison had rules that made bad behavior easy to punish.

5. **Based on the passage, which of the following statements is true?**
    - **A.** In the early years, inmates were allowed to talk only at designated times.
    - **B.** Many inmates escaped from Alcatraz over the years and made it to freedom.
    - **C.** Alcatraz was an inexpensive prison to run, compared to similar facilities.
    - **D.** Officials eventually found the bodies of Frank Morris and the Anglin brothers.

6. *Answer the following question using complete sentences:*
   Why do you think people are fascinated with the story of the escape by Frank Morris and the Anglin brothers?